True Tales of

A collection of original short stories

written and illustrated by Jim Molenaar

Forword

The best part of a memory is making it! -Unknown

Jim's stories call us back to simpler times and carry us through the trials and triumphs of family life and what it means to have a connection to the land. This small book of short stories is essentially a love letter to a life fondly remembered. Jim's gift is sharing true tales with humor and light, and he does it well.
-Heather Westburg King, Author, Flyleaf Bookstore Owner and New London Story Show director.

There are a few stories I always tell about the Tuesday Night Drawing Club, and Jim is in all of them. In 2018, I started a weekly schedule of teaching adults what I knew about establishing a drawing practice. We study the fundamentals of visual art, explore a variety of techniques and materials, and learn how to see progress in our own work. Jim joined early on with the goal of learning to draw 'just well enough' to illustrate his dad's stories. At first, he was cautious and tentative in his work. He had no confidence whatsoever – just the drive to get good enough to be able to tell the stories. The community we created within the club was what turned things around for Jim. He was surrounded by support, encouragement and recognition of what made his drawings so magical. We have watched Jim grow in his skills and fully inhabit the world of his stories. Jim is one of our group's shining stars, and it is an honor that we have gotten to witness his path to creating this book. The emotions he holds in these stories will be reflected in the images he has created. A treat for the reader only a writer/illustrator can achieve. Cheers from the Drawing Club, Jim!
-Kristin Allen, Artist and owner of Greenwater Garage and Gallery

If you grew up in the country, you know these stories. If you've never spent a day in the country, these are stories you should read.

A young man getting his first job because of his willingness to accept blame for a damaged car, a thirteen-year-old boy asking for skis for Christmas because if he could go cross-country he'd have extra time before school for chores, chores he needed to do because of the sudden death of his father. Another father lifting a car out of a snow filled ditch because that was the only choice he had.

These essays are the story of a man, a family, and a very small place, but in a larger sense they are stories of America. An America from a time and place that is often romanticized, with rough edges sanded down and a soft pastel sheen concealing reality. I understand the impulse to tidy things up, but it's a mistake, a mistake Jim didn't make. Jim Molenaar grew up in a place with the richest soil in the world that was strewn with rocks big enough to picnic on, with wetlands and prairie grass harboring a multitude of wild creatures. That's all gone now, rocks buried, and wetlands drained. The result is enough food in the world for eight billion people, but the losses are immense, and he doesn't pretend otherwise.

The stories span a hundred years or more, from ancestors crossing the prairie in a wagon pulled by horses to hysterically funny tales of camping adventures that are barely in the rear-view mirror. Tragic deaths and lives well led. This is a well-rounded view of humanity and life in the country.

Oh...and the drawings! Man, get the book just for the drawings!

-Brent Olson, Farmer, Big Stone County Commissioner, Awarded the 2024 Prairie Star Award from the SW MN Arts Council, 2014 Bush Fellow, A published author of the *Inadvertent Café and Between the Helpless and the Darkness* as well as writer of an on-line blog *Independently Speaking*.

1 THE OLD DAYS

My farmhouse bedroom where the stories truly began!

A common question in people's memoirs might be, "what is your earliest memory?" For me it involves sleep. My sister and I had a bunk bed in my mother and dad's bedroom. MaryBeth had the top bunk, and I was in the bottom. At age four I recall that I decided that it was more comfortable to sleep in the middle of my parent's bed than in my own bunk. After a few sleepless nights my parents decided that a better sleep option needed to be arranged.

The home I grew up in had an upstairs with a very steep staircase (more like a ladder almost) and an open space attic which was the underside of a steep Dutch inspired farmhouse. Holland was short on land and so homes were built tall and used as small of a land footprint as possible. My great grandfather brought the Dutch construction method to this spartan home. My parents began an intensive remodeling project of a dividing wall to create two bedrooms separated by shelves and a clothes closet. My sister's room was decorated in light blue and mine was red, white, and blue Americana. Wallpaper was applied and a layer of carpet was installed. The bunk beds were divided into two single beds. I was given a desk and small chair, which were painted in a red 'antique' style that matched the wallpaper. My desk was built by my grandfather Edwin using wood from an old trundle bed frame. The desk chair was brought from Holland by my Great Uncle William. It was done in the same style in an antique blue. Note: The chair and desk have been refinished to the original wood and now reside in my home.

The move in day and relocation to the upstairs seemed fun and exciting, to my four-year old mind. The first ritual was being tucked under the covers. Second came prayers, with both parents at my bedside. The words are easy enough to remember and we would say them together. "Now I lay me down to sleep, I pray the Lord my soul to keep. If I should die before I wake, I pray the Lord my soul to take." These words were then followed by more personal requests which I would make, "God Bless, Mom, and Dad, MaryBeth, Grandmas Ivel and Esther. God Bless (aunts and uncles) Vernon (Grace), John (Joan), Norman (Wanda), Gretchen (Roger), Doris (Irvin), Loretta (and Burton). God Bless, (cousins) Lynette, Patty, Dan, Becky, Joanie, John, David, Dawn, Greg, Lori Susan, Kent, and Jenny. God Bless John and Betty, Little John, Deb, David, and Tom." These prayers were followed by a resounding "Amen!"

The bless list was inclusive but not completely unbiased. For example let's just say if Cousin Tom had been unkind to me, he was dropped from the list. My parents usually caught the omission, "Aren't you going to pray for Tom?" and usually I grudgingly buckled. "Oh all right, God Bless Tom – even though he was mean to me today!"

At the conclusion of prayers I was given a hug and kiss from both parents, and they proceeded to head downstairs. Except that I was having none of it. "HEY! YOU CAN'T LEAVE ME UP HERE BY MYSELF!" Mom and dad explained that yes, that is exactly what they intended to happen. I created a fuss. My mother hit on the compromise idea that a bedtime story from my father might keep me under the covers. So began the bedtime ritual of dad telling me a story.

So what kind of stories you might ask? There were so many to choose from. For example, my older cousin Danny as a little boy kept telling my parents that he wanted "Cedar Shots." What was he talking about, my parents thought? Cedar Shots? Eventually it became clear he had watched my dad vaccinating piglets to prevent disease. He wanted to "see their shots!" Danny was a keen observer and he watched as my dad hand cranked the flywheel on the ancient John Deere 'A' tractor to start the motor. Later while in the house preparing for lunch, they heard the tractor start. They ran out to find five-year-old Danny standing proudly beside the running machine. Danny was very proud of his accomplishment. My parents were relieved that he was not injured by his tractor starting experience.

Nieces Patty and Lynette were always welcome with suitcases in hand to visit our farm. Warm memories retold often. My parents loved to recite the story of when I received a cowboy hat, boots, cap pistol and holster for my four-year-old birthday. "Take me to the barn, I want to shoot the pigs!" It was a fun recollection when I was young, a bit embarrassing when I was older. On April Fools Day I woke my parents in the early morning dawn shouting, "get up the cattle are out and on the front lawn!" Which they were not. I thought the prank was enormously funny. My parents did not appreciate my sense of humor.

My favorite stories were of my father's growing up years on the farm. Simple recollections of his youth, and memories of days gone by. The old times. The 1930's. I was fascinated. I could not get enough of them. I begged for more. Pleaded for more. Dad repeated the stories. I could not wait for bedtime. I made up names for each story. It was a bedtime ritual that started when I was young. It is surprising that I remember so many of the tales even now sixty years later. In 2012 my aunt Gretchen showed me a picture of my dad and brothers on a couch with a Rat- Terrier dog lying in front of them. "Oh, that's Zippy!" my aunt commented. I finally had a name to go with the tales of my father's beloved pet. Zippy adorns the start of each story of this book in a place of honor.

So I would beg to my Dad, "Tell me a story about the Old Days!" Those tales will be the focus of the first half of this book. The rest of the book contains the true stories of my own.

2 My Sense of Place

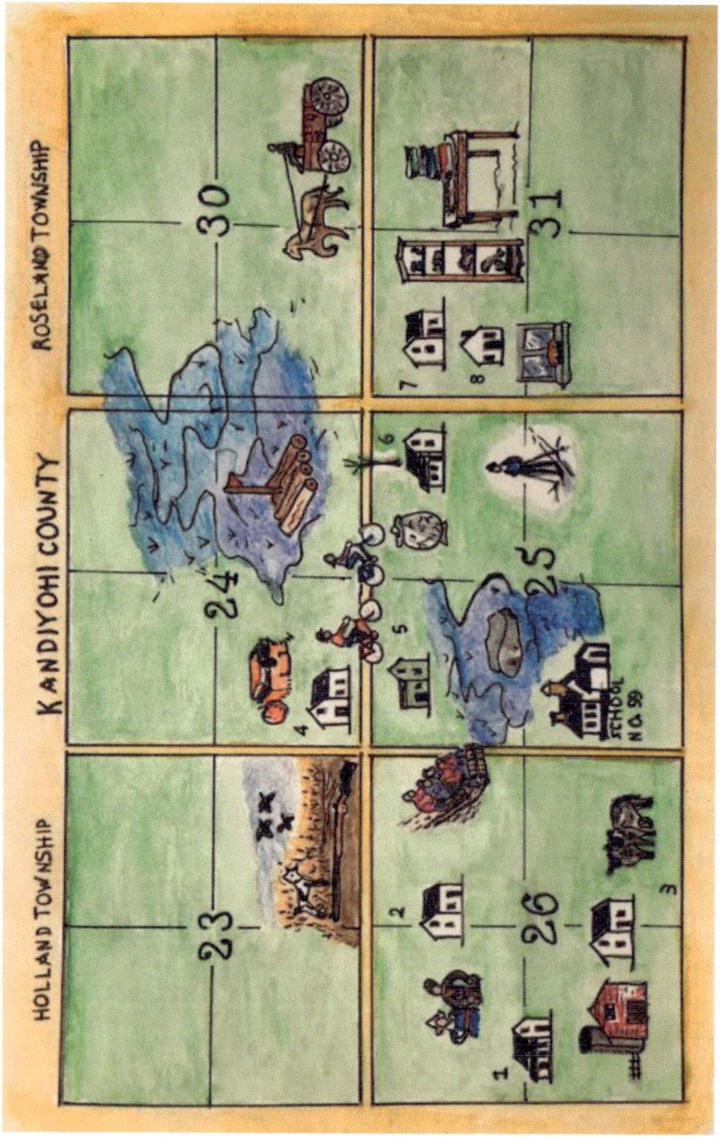

So many people and places to love!

Legend of the 1958 Plat Map

1 Klaas & Gretjie Molenaar (original homestead)
2 William (Bim) and Lizzie Molenaar
3 Clarence and Lena Molenaar (proficient cattle farmer)
4 Rueben and Kate Molenaar McClain (son Robert)
5 Harry and Harriet Molenaar (my sister MaryBeth and Jim "me")
6 Harry Sr. and Ivel Molenaar (later my uncle Vernon and Grace)
7 William and Nell Molenaar DeRuyter (Boulder Heights rock garden)
8 John and Betty DeRuyter (home of my childhood friend Tom)
* Nicholas and Grace Molenaar not pictured but 2 miles to the west
* Peter Molenaar (2 miles south and one to the west)
* John and Jenny Molenaar (near Kerkhoven)
* Robert and June Molenaar Schow family (5 miles due east)

Much of the Molenaar family history is recorded in a book titled A*ncestors of Klaas Molenaar and Grietje Zijp.* The history documents that they immigrated from Holland to Ellis Island, America in 1893. My grandfather Arien was renamed Harry as they are pronounced with much the same intonation. After a year in New York City they moved to New Brighton, Minnesota. Then in 1895 they located to their permanent homestead in Kandiyohi County where they farmed and raised a family. In this book it is stated, "Klaas missed all the relatives and friends in Holland. In America, he wanted his sons to be farmers and his daughters to marry farmers, so he continued to buy land close to his homestead so that his children would be near him."

By 1916 Klaas owned over 900 acres. He purchased most of this land for under ten dollars an acre. Today the same parcels of land might be worth over ten thousand dollars an acre and millions of dollars. My childhood home was part of this landholding. The farmstead was on the northwest quarter of section 25 in Holland Township of Kandiyohi County in the state of Minnesota. This farm was purchased in 1902 is now registered in Minnesota as a Century Farm, meaning it has been in continuous ownership by a Molenaar for over 100 years.

According to the Kandiyohi County History, if you were born in section twenty-five starting about 1800 and lived to the age of 220 you would have been under the sovereignty of Spain, France and the United States. You would have been a citizen of the territories of Upper Louisiana, Michigan, Iowa, and Minnesota. Then finally the State of Minnesota. You would have been under the local jurisdiction of Dakota, Pierce, Davis, Meeker, Renville, Stearns, and eventually Kandiyohi County.

I have illustrated a plat map for 1958, the year before I was born with a legend that lists the people and places that were part of the *Old Days* stories. Some of the farms do not fit on my plat map but those farms were relatively nearby. The miniature pictures drawn in – are my effort to depict some of the events and places that were part of my youth. It was a marvelous place to grow up. There were adventures galore in the grove with forts to build and old machinery to discover. The rock piles (long since buried to improve the farm) were places of adventure. We named specific large boulders based on the colors and lava intrusions that made them so interesting. In the 1960's prior to the farm improving tiling projects there were acres of large wetlands that sometimes were inhabited with waterfowl. Pheasants were abundant and usually came up to our farm site in the winter looking for food. It was easy to see the sunset with virtually nothing blocking the horizon to the west. Coincidentally there also was not much to block the bitter cold northwest winds that would rage across the winter prairie.

We had farm animals and pets. Close neighbors were mostly family members but there were also many friends. The Roseland Rosebuds 4-H Club was a big part of our social life with parents and kids joining together for education and fun. At the close of the school year in the first week of June many of the Roseland children were bused ten miles east to Big Kandiyohi Lake where we received swimming instruction. Believe me, the water was ice cold to our little bodies that early in the summer. Upon returning from the lessons we were able to buy a treat from the general store in Roseland. The three-room Roseland School provided education for grades one through four. My class numbered seven students but my sister's grade had only three pupils. After completing those grades we joined the big school in the town of Danube. My class of thirty-six seemed overwhelmingly large. I did not realize how intimate we were in that setting. Many of us are in close friendship now almost fifty years later. Our family did not have much, but we had everything that we needed. I shared so many adventures with my sister. My cousin Kent would come and spend the summers with us to get out of the city. He often talks about how those experiences still ground him. I got to live there. The farm still has a hold on my heart. It is my Sense of Place!

3 Building a Life and a Farm

The transformation of the original farm shack into a modern home was almost unbelievable!

My mom was born in 1923 to Edwin and Esther (Larson) Gadney in the farm home located in Lake Andrew Township of Northern Kandiyohi County. My father was born to Harry Senior and Ivel (Clough) Molenaar in Renville Minnesota in 1924. Dad's early years were lived in Renville where Harry Sr. was the manager of the Renville Cooperative Shipping Association. It is my impression that those early years of both my parents' lives were lived in relative 'financial' comfort. Maternal Great Grandfather Larson was a county commissioner. He was a respected farmer and owner of a prize stallion that was in high demand for his genetics. Harry Molenaar Sr. owned a Hupmobile automobile, and my father spoke lovingly of what was then considered a luxury car.

The depression was hard and unforgiving to rural and urban alike. For my Grandfather it resulted in the loss of his position as shipping association manager. Hard times created 'hard feelings.' I recall my father relating that Harry Sr. was a man of impeccable honesty and integrity. Even so his relative prosperity through the depression created jealous feelings among the farmers that he served. He was voted out as manager. This led to a move to the farm in Holland Township in 1934. Harry Senior was accompanied by wife Ivel, my father age 11, Vernon 10, John 8, Norman 3 and Gretchen age 2. Harry Sr. passed away in 1937 on a cattle buying trip in South Dakota, two years after relocating to the farm. From that time on my father was dubbed the 'man of the family' even though he was barely age 13. This is something that I have never been able to fully grasp, but more on this in my story the *Wishbook*.

My mom had a job working for the county and part of her responsibility was tagging the furs that trappers brought into the courthouse to receive a financial bounty. My dad's cousin Willard DeRuyter was an avid trapper and invited my dad along to redeem furs for a bounty. He introduced my father to a 'cute' girl who was behind the counter. A week later my Grandmother Ivel and my father appeared at the same desk to supposedly check on a drainage ditch assessment, which I think seemed a bit suspicious. My dad usually accompanied by one of his brothers drove north to enjoy the social activity of dancing. There was a pavilion in Spicer and on the next trip he spotted the "cute counter girl" and asked her for a dance.

Mom and dad were married in 1951. They chose to settle ½ mile west of Ivel's homestead in a house that had previously housed farm hired men. The home was built in the Dutch style of narrow and tall. There were a few trees, a small old pig barn and that was it. Really, it was very spartan even by standards of the early 1950's. They added a flat roof addition with a small entry way, a bathroom, and a bedroom to the original house. The original home was lifted, and a new poured concrete basement was installed under the whole setup. Barns, livestock, and trees were added over the years to become an operational farm site.

When you see the progression of the original shack to the flat roofed creation of master carpenters Harold and Virgil Harris it is really a change. An even more striking transformation came when my parents decided to remodel our existing home based on a house they had observed in a Duluth Park Point development during one of our family vacations. The idea was to create a roofline that could use the existing house, cover the flat roof with a conventional roof and create a better dining – living room area. All which would create a much more modern appearance. The carpenters hired to do this task were young and ambitious, but as I later learned inexperienced. This proved to be a critical complication to the project.

In order to remodel the existing roof they needed to first cut open the roofline and edges in order to attach the new structural timbers. With an injured leg in a cast that spring I did not have much to do other than sit in a lawn chair in a convenient location to observe the action. I watched with interest while my father reacted with alarm, that the carpenters left the roof open for the evening. My father recognized that a major rainstorm was imminent. We tried to add plastic covering but eventually gave in to the five-inch rainfall that literally soaked the inside of the existing home. It was surreal when I flipped the light switch in my bedroom to discover that the lampshade was filled with water. I thought to myself – “hey I have a built-in lava lamp!” I’m not sure what kind of accommodation the carpenters made for this disaster if any. My parents were patient and kind, and they diligently repaired the damage. When the project was complete my parents had a beautiful modern place to live and call home.

4 The Daring Hired Man

Joe Maats was truly a daring hired man!

I was particularly interested in the farming practices of my dad's boyhood. Among those was the harvest of crops. Farm work in the 1930s and 40s was nothing like what we see today. For one thing the harvest was particularly labor-intensive. Teams of men would come together to form a threshing crew. The farm women were very involved as well. Teams of men working physically required a large number of calories, so the women came together to prepare meals. I imagine there was some friendly competition to see who could make the best food or the most satisfying pies for dessert and earn the admiration of the working men.

One particular story captured my imagination then and still resonates today. Harvest was a time of hard work, but it also was fun in a way. Sometimes the older and younger men would compete to see who was stronger or smarter. Some of it was good natured ribbing or friendly sparring of words. I imagine it was just a great time for my dad to be a boy on the farm. Grain was planted in the spring and the wheat and oats were ready for harvest by mid-July. A team of horses pulled a machine that cut the grain and it was formed into bundles called 'shocks.' The shocks were each stacked on end in order that the grain could dry in the field. After a week or so of drying weather a team of horses pulled a wagon with sides (also known as a hay rack) and a man would pick up the bundles and throw them up and on to the rack. Another man on top of the rack would stack the bundles in orderly rows. The strongest and fittest men would do the throwing and the older more experienced men the stacking. It was important to do a good job so that the grain shocks did not fall off on the ride to the farm site.

Corn plants were also made into shocks when they became mature later in the fall. The corn stalks were made into bundles and after a brief time of drying they were transported to the farm site. Some of the corn shocks were chopped by a machine into small pieces of feed called corn silage. This moist product was blown up a pipe to the top of a silo. In the silo the corn compressed from its own weight and deprived of air it ensiled or fermented into a tasty nutritious feed for the cattle.

Harvest required many long days of hard labor. You could imagine the muscles a man would develop lifting shock after shock and throwing them over his head and trying to position them so that they would not fall off the rack. The unloading, storing, and subsequent feeding all required labor but also knowledge in order that the feed was made in a manner where it could store safely.

This reminds me of the silo and Joe Maats, my grandfather Klaas' friend and hired man. Joe was known to wear a bowler hat in a somewhat rakish style. Being a senior man on the worksite, Joe was assigned the important task of directing the silage spewing up the pipe from the blower. He would stand on top of the silo directing the spout to fill the silo evenly as the corn was blown out of the pipe. To get access to the top of the silo Joe would climb a narrow iron ladder up the side of the silo. It was a dangerous job as the silo was at least thirty feet above the ground. A fall would mean certain injury if not death. That fact did not seem to bother Joe. After each wagon was unloaded, there was a certain amount of wait time. This was when Joe would walk tightrope style around the top of the silo. The silo staves were roughly three inches wide. Using only his pitchfork for balance, Joe Maats made a circle of the silo top and then sit down on the precarious edge waiting for the next wagon to unload. After this tale I would ask my father breathlessly, "what would happen if he fell?" My father always replied with a chuckle that "He never fell, and that was a good thing too!" Joe was clearly cemented into history and my memory as the 'Daring Hired Man.'

In 1930 farm families were large because a labor force was needed to address all the work. An older agriculture teacher mentor explained to me that his high school average family size when he started teaching was almost twelve children. By 1970 the average family size had dropped to six. My grandparents Klaas and Grietje had eleven children. By comparison, my parents and most of my friends' families had only two or three children. Today both male and female farm operators can harvest more acres in a day than a 1930s farm operator could ever have imagined. It is a much safer and more efficient farming operation today, but it is also means less need for daring hired men and their courageous performances.

5 Fun on the Farm

Gretchen and Norman had stinky wet fun!

I was intrigued by what it was like to be a kid in the 1930s and 40s. I had my dad search his memory for examples. What did you do for fun? I was always entranced by his answer. It was clear that my dad loved his youngest brother Norman and sister Gretchen (In many ways my dad served as their father figure) and I could tell that their fun brought warm memories to him.

The kids had sleds made of two steel runners and a wooden platform which you could lay on, with a handle in front to steer. The best sledding hill was next door at the DeRuyter farm in Roseland Township. This was a short walk across the field to the east. The John Deere 'A' Tractor with a handyman loader attachment could make a tall pile of snow. The snow 'mountain' was a good starting point for the sledding run and the DeRuyters had a bit of a natural hill that was perfect for this fun. On cold nights they would pour buckets of water making an icy track for the sled runners. They would race down the snow pile and across the decline in elevation past the well pump, around the barn and off towards the grove to the Northeast of the farmstead. The steel runners polished with a bit of candle wax were daringly fast and both boys and girls spent hours enjoying this fun.

When Norman came down with pneumonia when he was young (I am guessing he was six years old) he was very sick, and the antibiotic treatments of today were not yet discovered. The only treatment was rest and so he spent most of his summer in bed recuperating. Vernon and John built a treehouse in the woods so that Norman could have a place to rest but also get out of the house. Crows were a menace on the farm destroying crops both in the field and in storage. They were considered a pest to be removed similar to how you might consider removing mice or rats from your home. Norman was provided with a single shot 22 caliber rifle (which is now in my possession in a case) and tasked with dispensing of any crow that came within a one-hundred-yard radius of his treehouse.

The big slough was located approximately one quarter of a mile northeast of the home farm. There was a huge rainstorm that turned the wetland into a giant lake. Norman and Gretchen found enough scrap wood to build themselves a raft. Somehow, they hauled their raft to the edge where they pushed it out onto the water. They then went swimming and enjoyed themselves on a hot summer day. According to my father the water was excessively stinky as shallow bodies of water filled with decomposing plant matter often can become. Gretchen and Norman were so odorous that they were required to wash off before they were allowed back in the house. An outdoor shower consisting of a black metal barrel on a stand with an attached hose was a rudimentary 'solar' shower. It was possibly a much preferable option to the indoor wash tub bath that would have been the alternative. Grandma Ivel kept a tidy house and I'm certain she wanted the mud and smell to stay outdoors.

When the old Hupmobile car was no longer useful as an automobile, brother John used the body parts to create a tree house in the woods. Using the seat, steering wheel, and some wheels from an old baby buggy he created a sort of play car. Wires connected the steering wheel to the front tires, which unfortunately were attached backwards. You had to turn the steering wheel left to go right and vice-versa. The car was put in motion by someone pushing from behind. I like to imagine that the car was indeed propelled by laughter! There were hideouts to be built in the hayloft and forts to construct in the grove. All great places for the children to read and expand their imagination.

My aunt Gretchen recounts that during World War II, they didn't have much but then they didn't realize it because everyone else was in the same place. She recalls that several cousins dressed up as patriots for the fourth of July Parade held in the nearby town of Prinsburg. Cousin Marjorie dressed as Betsy Ross of the Red Cross, cousin Donald was cast as Uncle Sam and my father wore a bowler hat and held a cigar depicting Winston Churchill. Together they marched in the parade and that no doubt must have caused a few chuckles if not out and out laughter. Perhaps the library book efforts of their Aunt Nell inspired them to recreate these characters? My aunt Gretchen recalls that there was a patriotic desire to serve by conserving food for the troops. This led to a national effort titled 'Victory Garden' where people were encouraged to raise as much of their own food as possible. This would serve the war effort by preserving as much quality food and supplies for the troops as possible. I was inspired by this effort and wish we could capture more of that sentiment today. What an amazing time to grow up, I think!

6 Gretchen's Rhubarb

Rhubarb crunch is served!

The county fair was coming up. In those days submitting baking for judging was a common activity. The problem was that during the depression years there were not a lot of baking products available on the farm. What they did have was a vigorous rhubarb garden, bulk bags of flour, and sugar courtesy of government surplus programs. That was all that was needed to make Rhubarb dessert. If you were going to submit something to the fair, you needed to practice or so Gretchen surmised. She began making rhubarb dessert. Rhubarb is fairly tart but if you add enough sugar, it can become edible. It was unimaginable to waste food and thus the Rhubarb dessert was served to the brothers for dinner, supper, and mid-morning or afternoon lunches. (Note here: City folk were often confused by the number of calories and meals farm workers needed for nutrition and safety breaks. The routine was breakfast, mid-morning lunch, dinner, mid-afternoon lunch, supper and finally a bedtime snack.) Gretchen experimented with a new recipe called rhubarb crunch. This was followed with rhubarb pies, rhubarb cobbler and more and more rhubarb. The brothers were willing participants at first. But have you ever heard the saying that when consumed in excess even the sweet begins to taste bitter? The brothers began eyeing the calendar and the realization struck that they had several weeks to go before the county fair. A strategy was needed. They hatched a plan to share as much rhubarb dessert with neighbors as possible. On further thought, anyone who drove on the yard was fair game for a rhubarb gift. Those gags aside, Gretchen was the pride of her older brothers, and they were pleased as can be when she earned a purple ribbon with her entry at the fair. Taste buds were protected and hurt feelings were avoided. All relations were seasoned with love, some amusement and behind the scenes fun.

My grandmother Ivel had a beautiful crystal cookie jar which she kept on the kitchen counter of her farm home. It was always stocked with wonderful sugar or peanut butter cookies for us to enjoy. Ivel was known to comment, "I kept a clear glass crystal cookie jar because I could hear when the boys would lift the lid (it made a clank noise) and I could tell if they were sneaking a treat." My sister MaryBeth and I were always welcome at her kitchen table for a cookie and a glass of lemonade. When we were old enough, she bought us each a bicycle so that we could ride from our home to hers (about a ½ mile trip) and visit her more often. We thought it was a great adventure to be able to go on our own to grandma's house and enjoy a treat. My father was moved to tears because he knew the financial sacrifices that his mother Ivel made in order to buy us those bicycles.

Another ½ mile to the east and we were at our great aunt Nell DeRuyter's home. Nell had a rock garden which she *called Boulder Heights*. The joke was that the soil of our townships were as flat as a pancake and thus her rock garden was indeed a 'height.' In order to grow her garden she had a deal with her boys which included my father and uncles. A nice flat limestone rock would earn the presenter a pie. You can bet they were all on high alert looking for rock pavers that would add to amazing *Boulder Heights*. She also had a curio glass fronted cabinet with a table beside it. This she dubbed her museum. She collected all sorts of fossils, bones, snake skins and collectable rocks. For us kids a pretty stone would earn a piece of candy. It was so much fun to spend time with these remarkable women, sharing a treat with my family on the farm.

We were always together, and food was a big part of family gatherings. Lutefisk was a definite no for my parents, and I don't recall that it was ever presented on the menu. Our county economic development director Wilt Croonquist once came to a meeting and expounded that he had prepared Lutefisk in his dishwasher. The high temperature and moisture environment was just what was needed to get the best whitefish he had ever eaten. The punchline was then delivered that he also needed to buy a new dishwasher the next day!

Swedish Meatballs, mashed potatoes, and gravy, krumkake as well as various Scandinavian cookies were all foods that graced the holiday table when we gathered at my aunt Doris' or Loretta's homes. My aunt Betty DeRuyter made the worlds absolute best pancakes – I think she used Crisco to grease the pan. Uncle John smoked and cured his own bacon. It was so salty and heavily cured that I think a slab of the pork hung on a barn wall would still be edible today. John and Betty were my dad's cousins, but we called them aunt and uncle out of respect. Believe me when I say that I had a deep respect for all you can eat pancakes and Uncle John's home cured bacon!

7 District 99

District 99 Schoolhouse mischief on our farm!

Federal legislation as a part of the *Homestead Act* required that land be set aside for the education of children. For every certain number of sections of land a parcel was required to have a schoolhouse for public education. On the very southwest corner of our farm was a white wooden rectangular building that housed school district 99.

Because my great grandfather Klaas owned much of the land within the boundary of district 99, it stands to reason that a significant number of the children attending that school were Molenaar cousins. Klaas was the school treasurer, and his son Cornelius was board chairman. Most of those cousins have gone on to have significant lives and made contributions to their community. As children I believe they were smart and creative within the confines of a one room schoolhouse. But cousins together are also bound to come up with some mischief. Those incidents provided my father with a source of humorous childhood stories.

When a particularly wet heavy snow hit, the boys got the bright idea to throw snowballs at the chimney of the schoolhouse. As they practiced, they became more accurate to the point which many of the snowballs hit the chimney top and went down. When enough of the snowballs contacted the hot wood stove at the bottom a fairly large puddle of water formed in the middle of the schoolhouse floor. The poor teacher was baffled as to the source of the unwanted puddle. The boys were also adept at removing the pins from the door hinges of the school. When the teacher opened the door to castigate the boys for some wrongdoing, the doors would fall off onto the ground. It must've been quite an event as I remember my father saying that the teacher held an inquisition, "all right who is responsible for this?" She received blank looks, and all cousins were able to keep their silence, with straight faces, and no one ever confessed.

Molenaar cousin Bob McLain's family must have had relatively good financial standing. When Bob received a brand-new lunch box for his birthday, he was the envy of the other kids. It was the spring, and the road ditches were running full of water. On the way home from school the boys would float their lunch boxes in the ditch. I guess you could call it a kind of a mini boat floating race. Most of the children's lunchboxes were black metal with a round top. Bob's box was painted with cartoons that made it different or better than what the other children had. There is a culvert that runs under the road near the school. On a dare it was suggested that if Bob's lunchbox was so good, maybe he could float it through the culvert under the road. Taking the dare his carefully launched box went into the culvert but did not reappear on the other side. I suppose the metal remains are still at their location under the road to this day.

One Christmas Bob received a beautiful new toboggan sled for his gift. When he brought the sled to school to show off, some of the girls began teasing and begging for a ride. The boys eventually relented and the girls' found seats on the toboggan. The boys mischievously gave them a hard push onto the ice of the nearby big wetland. The girls soon discovered that the ice did not support their weight and they found themselves standing in chest deep muddy water. A large boulder rock poked through the ice and the girls climbed on top and found themselves stranded with water on all sides. The boys found some boards and made a safe pathway for the girls to safely make their way back to dry land. The joke was on the boys as the teacher locked them out of the school for the afternoon in order that the girls could disrobe and dry their clothes in front of the stove. I met Bob McClain at a family reunion, and he really was a very likable man who had a successful career working for the Red Owl grocery store chain. I neglected to ask him if he replaced his lunch box or what happened to the toboggan. Some questions are better left alone.

It was a cold fall day in about 1965 when the schoolhouse was moved to a Lippert farm site about six miles away to become their family home, where it still is in use today. After the building was moved a bulldozer pushed the grove of trees into a large pile where hundreds of gallons of diesel fuel were applied to ignite a fire. My dad brought my sister and I to watch the burn on a cloudless extremely cold fall evening. I can still remember how numb my fingers were from the cold and the deep aroma of woodsmoke that saturated my clothing. It was the end of an era. There is a massive boulder rock which is the only remnant to mark the location of school house district 99. The rock will stay in its place of honor as long as the farm is under my sister's and my ownership.

8 Circus Riders

The boys were daring and creative!

Work horses were an integral part of life on the farm. By the time of my boyhood the farm work horse had been replaced by the tractor. Even so, I was fascinated with work horses and how they were used. Work was done with a 'team' of two horses. They were outfitted with heavy leather collars called a harness, and that was paired with various wooden poles and leather straps. All of which were attached to the implement that was being used in farm operations. Common farm field work included tillage of the soil in preparation for planting. Once the corn crop emerged the team pulled a cultivator to kill the weeds. This implement guided by a man, would eliminate weeds and push soil up around the growing corn plants. It was strenuous work on hot summer days. Later in the fall when the crop was mature the corn would be formed into bundles called shocks. The shocks would be loaded onto a horse drawn wagon and brought to the farmstead for storage. Finally the fields would be plowed as the final operation before winter.

My father explained what happened at the end of the day when the work was completed. As the horses neared the final 'round' of work for the day, Vernon, John and Norman would greet the teams as they reached the end of the field. The work implement would be unhooked. The boys were there and ready to assist the men by returning the team of horses to the barn. Walking and leading the team was an option. The industrious Molenaar boys came up with a better scheme. Horses were made for riding they presumed. Their first attempts brought the discovery that the work horse back was much too wide for a seated leg on each side position. In addition, the work horse gait was rough with much too much bounce to be even close to comfortable. Necessity is the mother of invention! The boys decided that they could stand atop two horses with one leg planted in the middle of the back of each horse. The reins would be held tightly and were a source of stability for the performer. There was quite a bit of trial and error, falling and frustration, until the process was perfected.

So here is how I imagine it. The men sweaty and tired reach the end of the field. Eager and energetic boys are on hand waiting and disconnect the team from the cultivator. Boy climbs to top of the team and sets himself ready for motion. Team is guided at a slow gait towards the driveway leading to the barn. Sensing that food and water are waiting the horses pick up their pace in ever increasing speed. The driveway corner is rounded, past a grove of apple trees, and the boy is desperately seeking balance to finish the trek home. The barn door is looming, and the team is now in complete control. I can still hear my father's voice as he reached the punchline. The barn door was tall enough for just the horse but not the boy. So the boys had to learn to time their daring ride and jump at the very last minute or they would crash into the wall of the barn. "What happened if the boys didn't jump" I asked with great earnestness? My father replied with a chuckle "well the horses always made it into the barn, but the boys never did!" It seemed so adventurous, wild, and daring. Just like the circus.

In the nineteen seventies my sister and I decided that we also needed a horse to ride. My father purchased Lilly, a Welsh Pony and she had a colt by her side named Cletus. The owner promised my dad that Lilly was as tame as a kitten and was so kind that she did not need a bridle but only a twine string around her neck. Translation. Lilly was as mean as a snake and when you tried to put a bridle on her she would rear up and try to trample you into the ground. If you managed to get her bridled, and you were on Lilly's back, she would race towards an elm tree in our front yard. The tree had a large limb at just the right height to scrape off a rider. It happened every time. Cletus was pretty but unbroken and wild. Dad hired a trainer who after several rounds of bucking bronco like maneuvers said, "that is not a horse for kids." Lilly and Cletus were sent to an auction house in South Dakota and that was the end of that experience.

Dad found another light tan, smallish horse, with a very wide back and a shorter body. We named her Queenie. She gave birth to a colt. The young filly was named Taffy. Queenie was afraid of cars and used that excuse to race out into the field and commence bucking until her rider was dislodged. She would then roll in the dirt. Queenie and Taffy had a habit of pulling out their tether stake from the ground to run away to the neighbors. Eventually my parents, my sister and I tired of the antics, and they were sold ending our circus. No one regretted the final act.

9 Picnic Rock

The Picnic Rock was a gift from the last glacier!

The picnic rock is a landmark on the flat fertile farmland of section 25, Holland Township. The last glacier deposited the deep soil but also a significant layer of large glacial erratic rocks that originated from Canada. On the west side of the farm was a large low area that formed a wetland. In the middle of the wetland was a large boulder which emerged or was covered with water depending upon the amount of rainfall received. You may recall the story of the toboggan and the big rock. This is a continuation of that story.

The Molenaar' s were industrious farmers and improving the land was part of their tradition. A bulldozer was engaged to push the large rocks into a pile or move them to a nearby line fence. When a caterpillar bulldozer began digging a hole to bury this particular large stone, a significant hole was dug. When the operator deemed it deep enough, he pushed the boulder into the hole. On this first try the rock was too tall and still stuck above ground level. The bulldozer pushed and pushed and eventually was able to remove the big rock from the hole. He then made numerous additional passes to make the hole deeper. Once again, the rock was pushed into the hole, and it was still too tall! The rock was removed again. The bulldozer made several additional trips down into the hole digging deeper and deeper. On a final pass, the bulldozer struck water and the hole began filling up like a swimming pool. That was the end of the rock burying hole digging process. Giving up the bulldozer pushed the rock across the field and placed it on the yard of the district 99 schoolhouse. My uncle Vernon who was generally a very serious man, related the story of the bulldozer and gave a deep humorous laugh in recollection. One of the Molenaar cousins inquired about purchasing the big rock to place in front of his lake home. My parents said that no, they thought the rock should stay as an icon and memory of days gone by. It remains in place to this day.

Sometime in the 1960's the schoolhouse was sold, and the small grove of trees were burned, and the land of district 99 became productive farmland. But both my father and uncle said that the rock should remain as a memory and marker of days gone by. The rock is large enough with a relatively smooth top perfect for my sister and I to have a picnic on top. Even the neighborhood kids took to calling it the picnic rock and it was well used. It is the perfect vantage point to imagine where the rock came from and where it will hopefully remain.

A bit more on the rocks of our farm. As the last lobe of the glacier retreated from our farm it left behind topsoil which it scraped from Canada and a less welcome deposit of rocks. There is a line from east to west over several miles where mighty boulders were deposited throughout the thick layer of rich earth. My father described it as thus. "When I took the tractor and mower out to a piece of pasture just west of our farm site, there were so many rocks that I was not able to even drive across the pasture, much less mow the grass."

Will DeRuyter used dynamite to split the large boulders into pieces. A team of horses could then manage the rock pieces as they were slid out of the way to a line fence or stone pile. My father and uncle hired a bulldozer to push the stones to manageable locations. With much expense, hard labor, and years of effort the boulders and rocks were removed from the tillable land and made into 'rock piles.' By the time my sister and I were old enough to play there were at least six stone piles on our two-hundred-acre farm. These piles with rocks much higher than our heads provided hours of entertainment and exploration for us. They also provided wonderful cover for small game and especially the ring neck pheasant population.

Rocks were a bane to farm equipment. When I overlooked a large rock due to inattention, I found the plow I was towing broken from the tractor and hanging on only by a few hydraulic hoses. On a different occasion my Uncle John Molenaar met the same fate with a field cultivator. He felt extremely bad that dad needed to spend a half day welding the hitch back together. When drain tile was added to the farm with a machine called a tiling wheel, the wheel would dig a trench so that concrete tiles could be installed and buried. The tiling contractor became extremely frustrated that he hit impassible boulders every several feet which meant removing the rock and restarting the process. These rocks added significantly to our stone piles. Modern farming practices dictated that these rock piles be buried. While this was very practical from an economic standpoint, I have a bit of regret that those glacial erratic piles will remain buried until the next ice age moves them once again.

10 Zippy

Zippy would wind his way through the tall slough grass!

Sometimes you learn parts of a story in spurts, and it takes time to pull all of those bits and pieces together. For example, I knew my father had a Rat Terrier dog. He spoke in loving terms of this pup. If he told me his name, I had forgotten it. Dad talked of taking the rat terrier hunting in the big slough just northeast of Ivel's farm site. It was the days before drainage and the area would have been a significant wetland. My father shared that the prairie grass back then was taller than his head. When hunting with my father in this area the smallish dog would wind his way through the grass seeking anything that would move. The Rat Terrior was relentless and although small in stature, he had the heart of a king. My dad explained, "he would wind his way back-and-forth, back-and-forth and all I had to do is follow along behind him." It is an image that has stuck in my mind. My father the boy winding his way through the wetland with his dog and probably not too many cares in the world.

A male dog will often lift his rear leg and mark his territory, which in this case the target was the nail bag belonging to the master carpenters Virgil and Harold Harris. The Harris brothers were building a barn on our farmstead. Later, after my parents married, the brothers did the construction of the addition to my parents' home. In the days before nail guns, the carpenters could add efficiency by filling their mouth with nails and spitting them out one by one to be hammered in. The carpenters were doing their thing, and the Rat Terrier dog was doing his thing, marking the nails. It was a collision course bound to happen. When the Harris brothers observed him peeing on the nails which they had been putting into their mouth, there was quite a bit of shouting and anger at the pup. I'm not sure how offended the Rat Terrier dog was, but what I do remember is my father's outright laughter when relating this story. Years later I ran into Jim Harris, the son of the skilled carpenters of this story. He asked me if the barn roof was still true and straight, as this was the mark of his father and uncles master building skills. I had to reply that yes the barn roof was as straight and true as a ruler, and the nails were still holding. I suspect that pup was proud of the part that he played in the construction.

Once on a visit to my Aunt Gretchen, she showed me a picture of three young boys on a couch in a posed picture that was obviously taken by a professional photographer. The boys are dressed in their Sunday best. Sitting in front of them is a small almost white dog with the right-side of his face and ear jet black. Upon further inquiry I learned that this was in fact the Rat Terrier dog that my father spoke so fondly of. Gretchen said that the dog in the photo was 'Zippy.' This knowledge pleased me to no end as it brought full circle the story of the infamous pet.

We had other pets growing up. I was really young, but I do have a vague memory of Scotty the Collie dog. Scotty was an outside dog and had a house immediately on the west side of our house. He was a kind and loving pet for us as young children. If he had a fault it was his propensity to tangle with skunks and his house was right below my parents' bedroom window. Our next dog was Erik a Norwegian Elkhound. The Elkhound is a smaller version of an Alaskan Husky with a tail that curled into an almost bowlike loop. Erik was gentle and was kind to all with one exception. You did not want to unroll his tail. Of course the tail was very compelling and invited a person to try just that. It must have really hurt because that would invoke a very serious yip and protective reaction from our kind pet. Erik loved to follow us to the school bus which picked us up at the end of the drive. On MaryBeth's first day of school Erik gleefully bounded into the bus with the apparent intent of also going to school. It took a bit of coaxing and embarrassment to remove Erik from his educational experience.

Dad had an old Dodge pickup truck we would often drive over to my uncle Vernon's farm site. Erik was always seated in the cab with us. On one such occasion he saw a rabbit in the road ditch. He chased the bunny by jumping out of the forty mile per hour pickup truck through the open passenger window. When Erik trotted back to the truck with tail held high, he seemed to say “Ha! I saved you from that one” and he was back to his perch on the front seat none the worse for wear. Erik was followed by Trigve, and he was the same breed and had the similar character as his predecessor. My sister and I also had a few kittens who were allowed to sit on our laps while watching TV, but they were never allowed to be fulltime indoor pets. Our farm menagerie was such an important part of our lives and oh how we loved them and the stories they inspired!

11 Long Tom & Hunting

The Long Tom provided a Grouse campfire dinner!

I was fixated on hunting and stories of hunting adventures. Changes in farming practices meant there was not a lot of hunting to be done by the time I grew up. Most of the wild areas were drained and tiled for modern farming usage. We had a wooden rack over the couch in our TV room. The first gun was a 22-caliber single shot rifle which my father said was purchased from the Sears Roebuck catalog in the early 1930s.The next gun was a Remington 12-gauge pump shotgun which could hold as many as six shells. This was a more modern weapon and the one that was used by my father to hunt. On the top shelf was a single shot 12 gauge with a broken stock and a very long barrel. It was named *Long Tom*. The *Long Tom* was noted for its ability to shoot the shotgun pellets a long distance in a very concise pattern with a lot of power. As my father noted you don't want to shoot that thing as it will knock your shoulder off. Family history records that the Schow cousins and my uncles went on a duck hunting adventure together sometime in the late 1930's. The Long Tom gun was mentioned that it was part of that hunting experience, however no mention was indicated if the boys found success. What is explained in the family history is that this specific gun was in the possession of my father Harry Jr. Molenaar. The stock was broken when my uncle Vernon noticed the conservation officer driving by when he was harvesting corn with the gun on the tractor with him. Of course this was very practical from a pheasant hunting standpoint but was also illegal. Vernon threw the gun into the standing corn to get rid of the evidence. He did not get ticketed, but the gun stock was found broken when he went to retrieve it. Having guns above our couch seemed very natural. We thought nothing of this arrangement that in today's society would seem out of place. It was very practical. The guns were tools. They needed to be stored somewhere, and the rack above our couch provided easy access to them when they were needed.

My parents talked of a hunting trip of newlywed couples to northern Minnesota for Ruffed Grouse. John and Betty DeRuyter were our neighbors and John was my dad's first cousin. They went on a hunting trip together somewhere north of Brainerd. Their canvas tent did not have a floor and all of the cooking was done over a campfire. My dad enjoyed this adventure, but my mom did not care for it. The Grouse hunt involved crawling on hands and knees through the brush to find the birds. I don't think this was my mom's idea of fun. But she did shoot a grouse as she wanted to please my father. She was a good shot and had a steady aim. A fact that was not lost on me!

As a boy, I vividly remember fall trips to Itasca State Park where we would camp and then drive the wooded roads of the area seeking the elusive grouse. I say elusive because I only remember one occasion where we actually bagged a grouse. We were often accompanied by my grandmother Esther or my great aunt Anna. Because my mom was afraid that we would become lost in the woods all of hunting was done from our car on gravel roads. There was a 'travel at your own risk' track through the woods titled *The Two Spot Trail*. It has now been abandoned to become a hiking trail which seems much more appropriate. A good thing as I recall that the Two Spot took the muffler off our car when jostling over a very steep and rocky path.

In the 1960s there were still many pheasants in the area around the farm where I grew up. There were brushy wetlands and grass for Ring Neck pheasant habitat. In the fall hunting season a lot of my parent's friends would come for hunting parties. In some cases it was as many as a dozen men. Two men would stand or post at the end of the cornfield. The other men would start at the opposite end and walk down the corn rows in affect flushing the bird. The men at the end of the field would shoot once the birds flew above them. I was not allowed to carry a gun, but I did get to walk along with dad. It was a totally entrancing experience for me. I couldn't wait for the day that I was old enough and allowed to carry a gun. Changing farming practices and some terrible blizzards in the mid to late 1960s decimated the wild game population on our farm which ended my opportunity to experience a pheasant hunt.

The guns are in my possession, but I rarely use them. They do provide some great memories of a time gone by. My friend the gunsmith Pat Laib, calls the old guns *Wall Hangers*, and I guess that will be their future place. If time and fate allow, I hope to repair the broken stock and have my friend Pat restore the *Long Tom* to its original glory.

12 Integrity

Treacherous ice provided a lesson about integrity!

When World War II was over Norman, John, and Vernon returned from military service to the farm. John and Norman had been stationed in Hawaii, but it was after the Japanese attack. My uncle Vernon was a member of the Merchant Marine delivering supplies to the troops in Europe. He told a story of traveling in groups with protection from gun boats. When the engine failed on his ship the pack continued on leaving my uncle's ship stranded without protection. When after three days the crew had repaired the engine, they managed to sail safely in to port. Uncle Vern shared that the crew of his ship fully expected that their lives were over in that experience. My father being the oldest was stationed at home on the farm to be the one who raised the food that the troops would need. The boys returned from the war. Vernon and my dad became partners in the farm operation. When it became clear there was not enough income to support additional families John and his new wife Joan moved to Rockford Illinois where he became employed as a machinist at Elko Manufacturing. The adventurous couple were very much a source of inspiration in their desire to travel and see the great sights of North America.

After seeing an ad in the newspaper for a job in Twin Cities Norman made plans to drive to Minneapolis for an interview. The day of the interview came, and it was a major sleet and ice storm. The roads and trees were layered with a coat of ice, and it was not safe for travel. Yet Norman was determined. In the borrowed family Chrysler Roadster car he drove to Minneapolis. He became disoriented and lost in his location. When he pulled into a parking lot of a factory hoping to ask directions, he lost control of the car which slid on the ice and hit a vehicle in the parking lot. Upon examination he realized he had damaged that car. He had no way of leaving a note so instead he walked into the office inquiring as to the ownership of the damaged car. He was told that he would have to talk Mr. Big (not his real name) he's the owner of this business and he is in his office. Norman went into the office introduced himself stating that he was very sorry that he had damaged Mr. Big's automobile, and he wanted to pay for the repairs. Mr. Big was very congenial, and he inquired of Norman "what in the world are you doing driving on such a terrible day like this." Norman replied that he was on his way to an interview at Western Union and that he didn't want to miss the interview as he needed a job having just returned from the war. "Who are you interviewing with?" inquired Mr. Big. He was elated to learn that he was good friends with Mr. Western Union. He then called his friend to explain that "I have a young man here who is on his way to interview with you, and I just want to tell you how impressed I am with him. He is a young man of integrity. He could've just driven away and not said anything after he banged up my car. But he was honest and came in and arranged to repair it. Mr. Western Union I suggest you hire him without hesitation."

Norman got to Western Union and had his interview. Before he left, he was offered a job. Norman drove home from the interview elated. I can just imagine the kitchen table scene with Grandma Ivel, Vernon, John, Gretchen and my dad sitting there. Norman's report of the fender bender, Mr. Big and the resulting job hire at Western Union was met with a great deal of congratulations. When Norman explained that his new job was the building elevator operator there were some good-natured chuckles. Norman had the last laugh. Even though the elevator operator was the lowest level job that a person could be hired for, he used the opportunity to introduce himself, greet and make conversation with each occupant of the elevator, many of whom were the chief executives of Western Union. Eventually those same executives saw the merit and potential of Norman. He was promoted again and again as he rose through the company ranks until eventually, he became one of the upper people in the Western Union Company. That is the story of how Norman came to be relocated to Middletown Ohio where he finished his career as a highly respected member of the Western Union Company. My father always made sure to point out that good things were likely to happen when you act with integrity!

My uncle Norman, Aunt Wanda and Cousin Lori Susan were favorites of mine and I always looked forward to a visit. Norman loved to take us to the Airforce Museum in Dayton. If you are interested in the history of aviation that place is a must see as it is near the field where the Wright Brothers perfected their first airplane. I marveled at the Kitty Hawk airplane on display and was wowed by a massive B-52 Bomber.

Norman missed the farm and hauled many car trunk loads of black dirt from our farm to his garden and even a couple of Colorado Blue Spruce Trees. He named two of them 'Harry and Harriet!' I like to think that they are trees with integrity!

13 Boulder Heights

The small cottonwood was the only tree on the horizon!

My great aunt Nell Molenaar DeRuyter lived just down the road from us. A smallish, but strong woman she was a source of inspiration and fun. Nell was smart, articulate, and really ahead of her time as a confident woman. She spoke with a Dutch accent that was no doubt a remnant of her childhood and ancestry from Holland. Nell was fond of relating that as a young girl when her family moved from town to the farm site in Holland Township, she rode in the back of a horse drawn wagon. As they rolled across the prairie there was nary a tree in sight. That is with the exception of a lone spindly cottonwood tree next to a large wetland. This became the home site of my grandparents Harry and Ivel. It was not much of a tree in 1902, but by the time I arrived on the scene in the 1960's the tiny cottonwood had reached mammoth proportions. Three grown people could not reach around its trunk. It was quite a specimen. It was hard for me to imagine a landscape with one tiny tree and nothing else but grass for as far as the eye could see.

Nell liked to teach about the soil of our farm. I can still hear her words in a distinct Dutch accent. "Look at this black earth. The deep dark color. Do you know that this soil is what brought us here from Holland? In some places this soil is six to eight feet deep. The glacier brought this soil all the way here from Canada. Then thousands of years of prairie grass, buffalo and fires developed the richest soil in the world." She went on to explain, "here, take a handful and press. Do you see your thumbprint in the soil? That means that it is clay-loam. Don't forget that this is the best soil in the world and our lifeblood. Respect this soil and it will take care of you."

The entry of her house held what she called her museum. It was a glass fronted curio cabinet with a wooden table next to it. She was interested in all things from the natural world. In her museum it was not unusual to observe fossils, bones, pretty rocks, and all sorts of wonderments. If you found an interesting rock, she would reward you with a candy treat from her jar. A large flat rock which she could use in her garden, would result in a pie made for the bearer of the stone. My cousin Deb DeRuyter Lippert recounts that Nell had an intact mouse skeleton and a snakeskin in the museum. Deb suggests laughingly, "they were obviously cherished gifts from someone, and they were clearly on display!"

Nell had a wonderful rock garden that was possibly thirty feet long by ten feet wide and as high as four feet tall in the middle. Hundreds of flat limestone rocks were arranged to hold soil in a mound which she called *Boulder Heights. Boulder Heights* was painstakingly arranged with a pattern of native plants and colorful flowers. While the surrounding landscape was as flat as can be, *Boulder Heights* was a fanciful and inspirational place to enjoy. A newspaper story reprinted in the family history book describes how Nell was instrumental in developing opportunities for rural children to have access to library services. The Willmar library did not allow rural farm children to use their books. So Nell made it her passion to develop a library for the farm kids. She was determined that her children would learn and be educated. When livestock was trucked to St. Paul to be marketed, Nell rode along in the truck. She made her way to the public libraries of the Twin Cities to ask for books to stock her rural library. She would spend the night in the truck as the livestock association bunk house would have been a man only experience.

This passion for learning and dedication to see that her children were educated can be seen in evidence throughout the subsequent generations of Molenaar/DeRuyter offspring. If Nell were living, she could count among her successor's medical doctors, nurses, aerospace engineers, teachers, environmental specialists, counselors, farmers and foresters. It all stemmed out of her deep passion for books and learning. Whenever I enjoy a piece of pie today in my modern life, I take a bite and smile with a bit of chagrin that I did not present a suitable rock to pay for the experience. Thank you, Aunt Nell, for this memory and please put a scoop of ice cream next to my slice of apple pie!

Son John and Betty DeRuyter lived in a small house on the same farmstead with Will and Nell. They were expert gardeners and horticulturalists. They had a row of apple trees lining the sidewalk up to the house. In their garden they raised the usual tomatoes, squash, lettuce, green beans and sweet corn. Those were all great vegetables, but my favorite was the watermelon and muskmelon that they produced. Uncle John would cut the muskmelon in half and fill its bowl with homemade vanilla ice cream. On a hot summer day after working or playing hard, that filled fruit bowl was a wonderful treat. John also had a smokehouse and cured his own pork including bacon. What fabulous people they were, and I was blessed to spend a great deal of time with them and my cousins.

14 Tornado

The boys headed for shelter when they saw the chicken fly!

The boys were out working in the yard; Vernon, John, Norman, and my father. It was a hot humid day and dark ominous clouds began forming in the west. I am certain that everyone on the farm was aware that a storm was coming. An emerging funnel cloud caused the boys to race for the house. Imagine their consternation when they realized that their mother Ivel had blocked the door with a chair. She was afraid that the wind might break the door or cause some other form of destruction. The boys turned and ran for the large livestock barn. When they observed a chicken being sucked up into the funnel cloud, they realized that it was going to be a serious storm. From inside the structure my father recalled his father's sage words, "never go in a barn during a tornado!" So wisely the trio sped across the yard to the chicken coop which was located immediately to the west of the house. The tornado struck with full fury of wind and sound. The barn did not survive, and it collapsed into a pile of debris. The top of the concrete silo was demolished, and the adjacent windmill was crumpled into a pile of steel. Much of the steel roofing and lumber ended up wrapped around trees a quarter mile east at the DeRuyter farm. When the storm passed and the boys emerged from the chicken coop, they were thankful to God that they had not been in the barn. At this point in the story my father would again emphasize to me, "do not go into a barn during a tornado!"

I remember observing a tornado when I was a student at Willmar Community College. During a night class sudden high winds broke the doors and glass of the science building. Class was canceled and we were all sent home. That same evening I remember sitting outside on our farmstead watching with concern to the northeast as I observed a funnel cloud traveling across the land. That tornado was probably 5 miles away. What I vividly recall is the dust the funnel cloud created and a sudden burst of boards and debris that were cast into the air as it hit a farm site. No one was injured thankfully and that was a fortunate thing.

July 1 of 1981 I began my first teaching assignment in St. Peter Minnesota, and I truly missed the farm. At that time phone calls were all landline and long distance – if you could catch the person at home. My cousin Kent Rasmussen, seven years my junior, was spending the summer months at the farm with my dad. He was enjoying that I was away, as he got to do all the farm tasks that had previously been mine. Operating the Bobcat loader, driving the feed tractor, checking the crops, feeding the animals and so on. My dad loved him, and they were best of friends. All of my cousins are important to me, but I consider Kent my brother and he was the best man at my wedding.

One day a storm with deep dark clouds formed to the west of our farm. Out of those clouds came a hailstorm that was so intense that when the fury had passed the hail essentially shredded any semblance of the beautiful crop that had been present. In tears Kent called me and sobbed "Jimmy, the crop is all gone. The hail ruined the crop and there is nothing left. Uncle Harry, Aunt Harriet and I don't know what to do. What are we going to do?" I did not know what I could do but experience the pain of loss with them even though I was over one hundred miles away.

I recall a strong thunderstorm with an eerie greenish yellow sky. A hayrack wagon on our yard was literally blown several hundred yards until it came to rest against a hedge. Several wagons were tipped on their sides. The nice, neat rows of wheat waiting to be harvested were scattered across the field. A late summer thunderstorm leveled our fields of corn as if they had been flattened by a steamroller.

These weather events were a vivid reminder of the fury that can be created from our atmosphere. Perhaps this is why we Minnesotan's spend so much time listening to predictions, listening to the radio (especially for blizzard related school closings), looking at our iPhone, and of course talking about the weather. I have heard people from Coastal California complain that the weather is the same every day of the year. I suppose that could get boring. Our climate certainly is not dull. A true

Minnesotan is likely to say, “Don’t like the weather we are having? Wait a minute and it will get worse!” This was evident in my father’s story of the crumpled windmill, demolished barn, shredded crops and damaged machinery. All were a visual reminder of a storm’s power. Many of these artifacts were still present well into my youth. The drama of the bedtime story clearly made an impact as today I am very mindful of the weather. I hope the reader will forgive me if I repeat my father’s words, “Never go into a barn in a tornado!”

Final note: When slightly before publishing, I shared this story with May DeRuyter Bottke. (daughter of Nell in these stories) She replied, “that tornado happened on September 6th, 1942. I know that date because it was my first day of college.” What a remarkable lady to have that clarity of memory at age 98! I am proud to call my father’s cousin my ‘aunt’ out of respect and love.

15 Electricity!

Rural electric was a life changer on the farm!

I was particularly fascinated with my father's life growing up on the farm. For instance, in Grandma Ivel's basement there was an access door with a chute leading to a coal burning furnace. My father explained that coal would be delivered on a truck, slid down the chute into the basement for storage and shoveled into the furnace during the winter to heat the home. During World War II when coal was scarce, corncobs and even cattle dung were burned for heat. I grew up during the time of instant heat from a fuel oil furnace. Today I am connected to the convenience of natural gas for heat and hot water.

My dad recalled that electricity was brought to the farm via the Federal Rural Electrification Initiative. Poles and wires were installed in 1939. This meant electric light and the convenience of indoor plumbing- eventually. This brought many questions to my mind. What did you do for light? How did you take a bath? Where did you get your water?

My father's answers were always provided with a lot of patience. He responded that before electrification they used oil lanterns and candles for light. They had a metal drum on a wooden stand out in the yard. The drum was painted black and held about 40 gallons of water. The summer sun would heat the water and a hose coming down was used to take a shower. The water came from a well pump out near the barn which was connected to a windmill. Every morning one of the siblings would go out and capture a bucket of water that could be used for cooking, washing hands and household needs. The bathroom was an outhouse with a pit. Toilet paper was not readily available. A Sears Roebuck catalog or even a bucket of corncobs were very useful items for hygiene if you understand what I am saying. What about the winter? I was old enough to realize that outdoor showering was likely not an option for at least six months of the year. My father responded "We had a tub in the dining room filled with water we carried in and heated on the wood stove. We bathed, once a week on Saturday night to be ready for Sunday church." Youngest first and on up the line to my father who was last.

What about food? How did you store your food? How did you cook? The answer was canning by storing the food in vacuum sealed glass jars. The stove was fueled with wood and water was heated in a kettle on top. They bought dry food and much of it was in cans. Meat could be kept fresh and frozen during the winter. Some was smoked and salted for preservation for the warmer months. People had small shacks where they kept blocks of ice covered in sawdust and preserved for the summer months. I don't think the Molenaar's lived in close enough proximity to a lake to enjoy that amenity.

My father recounted that a highlight of his youth were occasional Saturday trips to the town of Thorpe on the *Loose Line Railroad. The Loose Line* was lovingly dubbed *The Tooterville Trolley*. The railroad ran from the town of Bunde twenty miles to the west and continued all the way to Minneapolis another one hundred miles to the east. The nearby town of Roseland had a train stop and the Molenaar kids could travel east twenty-five miles to the town of Thorpe. My father's aunt and uncle Howard and Ella Clough owned and operated a general store in that town. The weekend trip to Aunt Ella's meant a choice of boxed breakfast cereal from the store shelves. This was considered a big treat. The farm menu generally only provided bulk malt-o-meal or oatmeal for breakfast cereal. In the 1960's what once was an essential transportation link became obsolete as highway development and truck transportation replaced it. Today the eastern portion of the Loose Line has been developed as a recreational bicycle trail. Points west were converted back to farmland.

If I close my eyes and think of my grandmother Ivel's home, I see a lovely claw footed dining room table with chairs and an ornate beer stein on a shelf that my Uncle Vernon bought in Germany following the war. I can almost smell her Christmas evergreen tree. She adorned it with real candles, popcorn and cranberries which my sister and I were recruited to string. Her beautiful collection of glass ornaments twinkled and reflected light in a multitude of directions. It was a magical place for us to visit and her home was filled with love and merriment. Life was not always easy, but I recognize how much joy was present at the homestead even prior to Rural Electrification. I can still hear the clink of her cookie jar and the sound of lemonade being poured into my glass at her kitchen table and those memories do not require an electrical plugin.

16 Tractor Race!

The model 'B' John Deere and my father were the winners!

I recently rode in a combine that was equipped with the latest in modern farming technology. Steering was guided by a satellite. A monitor reported real time yield, moisture, and grain quality. All of this information was digitally recorded on an electronic map. Corn yield readouts suggested somewhere between two hundred to three hundred bushels per acre. The combine would unload into a massive grain cart pulled by a four-wheel drive tractor which in turn unloaded into a convoy of three semi-trucks. The grain was transported to a 'condominium' in town where it would be stored along with grain from other farmers in the area. It was a well-orchestrated and planned harvest. A massive 650 horsepower four-wheel drive tractor followed the combine tilling the soil to prepare for next year's planting.

My father's experience was very different but no less exciting in my eyes. He told this story with a twinkle in his eye. In 1938 my father and uncle Vernon bought tractors to replace the work horses that had been previously the primary workforce of the farm. A one year used John Deere 1937 model 'A', a brand new 1938 'A' and three years later a 1941 John Deere 'B' were purchased. The 'B' sported possibly fifteen horsepower and the model 'A' came in at a whopping twenty-six. Just for comparison sake I want to profess that my riding lawnmower is rated at twenty-two horsepower. The comparison boggles my mind.

My father had made a trip into the town of Roseland with the recently purchased 'B' John Deere tractor pulling a wagon. On the return trip he found himself sharing the road with neighbor Calvin Damhoff who had a recently purchased 26 horsepower red Farmall 'H' tractor. Red against green! Calvin made a move to pass my father with the more powerful and supposedly faster machine that could sport a top speed of sixteen miles per hour. This was when my father delivered the punchline. "I had the throttle pushed to the maximum speed, 15 miles per hour, and I was losing ground. But down below the dash was a spring that connected to the throttle. By pressing that spring with my foot I managed to get a burst of speed enough that I was able to go right on by Calvin before he reached his driveway!" I cheered the win and shared the pride of a young man in a moment of triumph.

The love of tractors may seem strange to a person that did not grow up on a farm. I found real joy in each piece of machinery. In my younger years I had the opportunity to drive the older model tractors as they were deemed safer due to their simple design and operation. By the time I hit junior high I was in full mode of cultivating corn and hauling manure with the sixty-horsepower model 720 or 730 John Deere diesel tractors. The engines on those two tractors had a piston about the size of a coffee can. The engine rumble was clear and powerful. Their deep rumble could be heard across the countryside, and I loved them for it.

My cousin Kent would spend his summers on the farm learning about farm life and spending time with my dad. His mom Gretchen related to us that most of his friends and city kids would have a very smooth 'purr' noise when they were playing with toys. Kent came home with a very clear John Deere 'put-put-put' sound that he learned from listening to the old two-cylinder tractors.

In 1973 my dad and uncle had a good year as did many farmers. Grain prices were up due to a big sale to Russia and the yields were also strong. They decided to upgrade to a more modern tractor with greater horsepower. Every other farmer had the same idea and there were no John Deere 4020 tractor models available on machinery lots. Fuller Implement in Renville Minnesota had an 856 International Harvester for sale which was the red equivalent size of the green JD. It was twice the horsepower of any tractor we owned, and it had a cab with a heater. With powerful headlights it was easy to do the field work of plowing and cultivating the soil at night. The green and red dashboard lights were so very strong and cool. I would drive the tractor well into the night just for the sheer enjoyment of it. I might have done better than 4th in my class had I been more diligent, but my plans were heavily invested in farming, and I loved it!

It is a mind-blowing experience to compare what a modern farm tractor can accomplish in terms of sheer power and efficiency compared to my generation, but even more so to my father's time. Even so, I have to imagine that the thrill of the tractor race would be hard to top in terms of sheer pride and enjoyment. Today if I am driving on county road five just south of Roseland, I am tempted to push the foot pedal just a bit harder and wave a checkered winner's flag at the memory!

17 The Blessings.

The doctor lit a firecracker to celebrate the 4th of July and my mother's birth!

Mom presented both my sister and I with a book of memories titled *The Blessings of My Life.* I treasure this book as it is a remarkable account of her life. Agnes Harriet was born to Esther and Edwin Gadney on the 4th of July 1923, at home on the farm located just off the Little Crow Trail, eleven miles north of Willmar. Mom liked to remind us that soon after she was born, the doctor "shot off a firecracker on the back porch" to announce her arrival. Her parents told her that she jumped in her bed – confirming that her hearing and reflexes were good! Her name was chosen to honor her Aunt Agnes who fell ill and died from the 1917 Spanish Flu on her honeymoon. At her baptism, the pastor said, "I suppose you will call her Harriet" and that is the name we all knew her by.

To say that family was important to mom, would be an understatement by far. Both of mom's sisters were also born in the farm home. Doris in 1925 and Loretta 1928. Mom wrote that they were each other's best friends. There was not a lot for entertainment of the farm, but they enjoyed each other's company both in childhood and throughout their entire lives. Doris married Irvin Swedburg and Loretta to Burton Brant. My Aunt Loretta once commented to me that it was important to be together at least every Sunday, year in – year out. "Many times we would risk travel in snowstorms or worse – to be together."

In her early years, Mom managed to secure work for Kandiyohi County doing clerical and whatever needed doing, including punching the ear of dead stinky animals that the trappers brought in. It was not fun and it seemed that the men of the office were always missing when a trapper threw a dead fox on the counter. She laughed, "The job was left to me!" Willard DeRuyter Jr. told my father that he'd like to have him meet the girl that had to do this job. So one day my father accompanied his cousin Willard to the office. A week later, dad and his mom came in to check on a ditch lien (very suspicious I think) which was also one of mom's responsibilities. Shortly after that, they met at the Dance Pavilion in

Spicer, where dad asked mom to dance, and then again and finally if he could give her a ride home to Willmar. That was the beginning of their dating life, Tuesday night dances in Spicer, and lunch at John's Supper Club on the way home.

Mom and my dad, Harry Molenaar were married on February 3rd, 1951, at the Covenant Church in Willmar. The winter of 1951 had seen record snowfalls and drifts along the country roads in Holland Township. Fearing that dad would not be able to get out to the wedding ceremony, Mom called her friends at the county highway department. A convoy of bulldozers and snowplows were dispatched to clear a path for dad to get to his wedding ceremony. Mom liked to tell later that the snow patrol guys would tease her by saying "Harriet, we had to get Harry out, otherwise how were we going to get rid of you." Mom and dad had a wonderful honeymoon to Southern California, and they returned to MN a month later to, you guessed it, a March 1st blizzard. That same winter Betty DeRuyter needed to get to the hospital to deliver Johnny. She stood holding the sides of a flair box wagon while in labor. The wagon was pulled by a caterpillar tractor two miles to a more improved highway and a car!

Mom also related the interesting experience of watching the CCC workers developing Sibley State Park. On a Sunday afternoon the Larsen/Gadney family would load up in their model 'A' car and drive through the camp where the workers lived during the park development. She recalls the memory of many butchered chickens hanging from a clothesline waiting to be turned into dinner for the men of the camp. The CCC builders were master stonemasons and had already had experience developing other parks including my favorites of Gooseberry Falls and Itasca State Park.

After her father passed away the responsibility of driving the family car fell to the oldest, my mother. She tied a box to her foot so that she could reach the accelerator, clutch, and brake pedal. On many Saturdays the Gadney's drove to the train station to pick up a pastor who would be speaking at the Lake Florida Mission Covenant Church on Sunday. They would feed and house that person and return him to the train on Monday. It may have been a challenging lifestyle, but my mother counted each day as a blessing when she could be with her family.

18 Harriet's Tales

The big fish got away!

These were mom's stories. She could tell them well and she recorded them in a book of her memories.

Careful Harriet: A trip to California with Cousin Norma and Doris. To say that Doris, Norma, and mom did not have much money was an understatement. But somehow, they planned and went via bus and train to Southern California. The trip included San Francisco and the redwood forest. It was the trip of a lifetime. On the return trip, they found themselves stranded in Kansas City. The problem wasn't that they did not have enough money, they had no money! Mom said that they could not buy food and were hungry. She said that all Norma could do was 'giggle' and that Doris was upset and did not know what to do. Mom had a checkbook from the Bank of Willmar and decided it was her job to get their hotel to cash a check. She convinced the hotel management of her honesty. They allowed her to cash a check and the trip was completed.

The tomato and deadeye Harriet: Mom and dad raised free range chickens, before people even knew about free range chickens. They also had a mean rooster. It once chased mom, and we kids were not allowed out to play if the rooster was in the vicinity. Mom had been growing a tomato plant, watching a particular tomato for several weeks, waiting for it to ripen enough to eat. The rooster had been watching too, and just as the tomato was deemed ready to pick, he pecked the tomato and turned it into mush. There was a single shot 22 rifle, on the rack in our family room. Mom took the rifle and dispatched the rooster with a single shot – right through the eyeball! Those of us around mom, had a newfound respect, as the rifle was right there on display in our house for all to see!

The Big Fish that got away, and one that didn't: My dad loved to fish. Mom loved my dad and began to enjoy fishing with him. On one particular trip – with friends Wayne and Jean Bennet on Burnt Lake near Ely, mom caught a large fish. I don't know what type of fish, but it reportedly was big. In trying to remove the hook, somehow the fish got away from dad. It flipped out of the boat, and back into the water. This somewhat upset my mom. Later that night as mom was dreaming, she got her arms around dad's leg in a death grip and reportedly called out, "you're not going to get away this time!"

My mom was very close to her sisters, but also had two good friends in Phyllis Williams of Roseland and Dorothy Ledeboer of Prinsburg. There were other acquaintances of course but those two were the closest. The connection with Phyllis was through having children roughly the same age. Mom and Phyllis enrolled in an oil painting class and that led to a lifelong friendship. Mom did some wonderful paintings of our farm and one especially wonderful rendition of the Split Rock Lighthouse. The Williams kids were part of our 4-H club, and we were good friends. Dorothy's children were Judy, Rod and Kerri. Rod worked for my dad on the farm during his high school and early college years and Kerri was one of my sisters' close friends. Rod and his buddies asked dad if they could have an old 1940s Plymouth car that was abandoned, mouse infested and parked in the weeds next to our shed. Those boys got that hot rod car running and bombed around Prinsburg with it for many years. My father always had a heart for young men, and I think it gave him great pleasure to see the derelict car on the road again.

The Lake Florida Church was a center of my mom's family growing up. The church discontinued regular services in the 1950's and now has an annual reunion service on the first Sunday of August. I was honored to be asked to speak at the one hundred and twenty fifth anniversary celebration of this church. My mother and father are interred at Lake Florida Mission Church, next to my mom's parents and grandparents. The pastor who spoke at my mother's funeral explained that the ancient Israelites sought high elevations, with available water and shade to create their places of worship. Today the rolling hill is surrounded by trees, but in the early 1900's you could see the wetlands to the east and the horizon in the west. In my opinion the church grounds and cemetery are the most picturesque view of wild lands in the county. I agree with the pastor that the Lake Florida Church exemplifies all of the attributes of a holy place. Mom bought burial plots for my sister and I, including our spouses. I suppose that will provide my final resting place as well.

19 The Yellowstone Trail

Yellowstone Park was the adventure of a lifetime!

I can imagine the level of excitement that happened when the Yellowstone Trail Highway number 212 passed through my grandparent's hometown of Renville. My grandmother Ivel loved to travel, and she often stated she was certain that somewhere in her heritage might have been a genetic tendency for travel and adventure. This fact aligned with my grandfather's work as the Renville cooperative shipping association manager and the marriage of Ivel and Harry Sr. Molenaar in 1922. Harry Sr. would have been accustomed to railroad trips west to buy calves from Rancher's in the Dakota's and western Montana. My grandfather also had the means to purchase a new Hupmobile auto. In 1920 a new Hupmobile would have listed for $1,250 which would have been a large sum at that time. Created by Joseph Hupp the auto was considered state of the art with all steel body construction and a powerful engine. It is then no surprise that my grandparents along with oldest brother and wife John and Jenny Molenaar, decided to travel by auto to Yellowstone National Park for their honeymoon in 1922. My aunt Gretchen explained that it was not unusual for a couple to have others join them on their honeymoon trip in that time. It was a six-week journey, and its length astonishes me.

The Yellowstone Trail was the first transcontinental auto route through the northern tier of states. In 1912 it was initiated by a conference of businessmen in Ipswich, S.D., under the leadership of Joseph Parmley. The group wanted to build a better road between Ipswich and Aberdeen 26 miles away. The endeavor began the Yellowstone Trail, which would soon stretch coast-to-coast, from Plymouth Rock to Puget Sound. It thrived because of the cooperation of thousands of grassroots supporters.

The trip west was by no means an easy one, the roads would have been dirt or at best gravel along the trail in 1922. To develop the road, 'Trail Days' were held with picnics to make the work of 'dragging' the dirt road more fun. The Yellowstone Trail Association had local chapters in towns and state chapters to oversee routing. Railroads had already selected the most efficient routes and local roads already existed near the right of way; so as one reads the history of the Yellowstone Trail, one also reads the history of the Milwaukee Railroad. In today's travel of Interstate Highways, the trip across South Dakota is not necessarily one that is particularly interesting, though I admit there is beauty in the great plains. But imagine traveling across that vast prairie on a gravel road at a top speed of twenty miles per hour. No wonder the Molenaar journey spanned six weeks of time.

The first point of interest on the journey might have been crossing the continental divide at Ortonville. This is a separation of the Minnesota River flowing to the south and the Red River flowing to the north to Lake Winnipeg. Another two hundred and fifty miles to the west the travelers would have approached the Missouri River crossing at Mobridge South Dakota. A single lane pontoon bridge crossed the wide expanse of water. It was at best a questionable crossing. A new suspension bridge would not be constructed at this location until 1924. Brother (Bim) Will Molenaar was deathly afraid of bridges, and he had an expectation that they would collapse while he was traveling over them. When crossing a bridge, he would open the door of the car and hang his legs out in order that he could jump to safety if necessary. Did the Molenaar party cast a chuckle thinking of Bim as they passed over the mighty Missouri? Likely they did, even though no such calamity occurred on this journey.

Further travel would have led our newlyweds across the Southwest corner of North Dakota and on into Montana. Our travelers would have marveled as they came alongside the Yellowstone River. The trail would follow the river west to Billings then on to Livingston and Gardiner. A grand archway entrance of field stone would have greeted our travelers at the North Entrance to Yellowstone National Park. It was at this location that President Teddy Roosevelt dedicated the park. It would have been an amazing sight then, and it still is impressive today.

Yellowstone National Park was created in 1872 and was approximately 62 miles long and 54 miles wide. The area of the park is 3,348 square miles or 2,142,720 acres. Over 85 per cent of this great parkland is covered with dense forests of pine, fir, spruce, and other trees. Prior to 1915 the only travel in Yellowstone National Park was by horse. In 1922 my grandparents would have been able to drive the park with their Hupmobile, however the trip would have been no easy journey. Travelers were advised to adhere to speed limits of 12 miles per hour ascending and 10 miles per hour descending steep grades and no more than 8 miles per hour when approaching sharp curves. On good roads with straight stretches and when no horse team was nearer than 200 yards, the maximum limit was 25 miles per hour.

Their first stop was likely the central information bureau and headquarters at Mammoth Hot Springs. Here also was the park museum and library. Maps and other publications could be obtained at this office. The national park map and travel information suggested that a visitor should insist that the driver stop at all points on the loop road system which were indicated by an arrow. The information would have suggested that Yellowstone National Park was an ideal vacation resort. It was considered worthwhile to spend a week, a month, or, indeed, the entire park season.

They would have made stops to see Camp Roosevelt, Yellowstone Lake, and River. Almost certainly they made a visit to the Old Faithful Geyser and Mammoth Hot Springs. The Grand Canyon of Yellowstone and the spectacular falls of the Yellowstone River at that location are marvels even today. Visitors who were seeking rest and less strenuous recreation were invited to visit the natural hot Sulphur baths. There were four hotels in the park maintained by the Yellowstone Park Hotel Co. They were located at Mammoth Hot Springs, the Upper Geyser Basin, the outlet of Yellowstone Lake, and the Grand Canyon of Yellowstone. In addition, Camp Roosevelt Hotel provided an iconic location to enjoy the

Northeastern corner of the park. The Molenaar travel party would have paid for meal and lodging $6.50 per day with an additional $1 per day for a private bath. Meal and tent lodging would have cost $4.50 per day.

The trip home likely was equally challenging. Often the reverse trip home is not as exciting as when you are heading to your destination. Yet there were rivers to cross, rutted roads to traverse. My grandfather loved cattle and I have to imagine he enjoyed seeing the open range. Did they stop to visit with people along the way? No doubt, they had great tales to tell when they returned to Minnesota and the farm.

It was an adventure of a lifetime, and I have enjoyed re-creating their travels. It is not hard to imagine that the same adventure gene that inspired my grandparents is also present in me enough that I hope to visit all of the national parks in the lower United States in my day. Even so, I cannot dream that I will top the honeymoon of a lifetime!

Postscript to the story: The Hupmobile clearly made the trip home with flying colors. I know this because my father pointed out a vehicle transmission that was stashed in our grove. “That came out of the Hupmobile” he told me. The running gear under a hayrack was made from the frame of the Hupmobile. My uncles John and Vernon created a tree house in the woods using the body parts from the vehicle. The seat was recycled as a part of a pushcart that provided hours of joy to my uncle Norman and aunt Gretchen. It was an amazing car providing an inspirational journey to a couple of newlywed adventurers!

20 The Wish Book

The Sears & Roebuck Wishbook was eagerly anticipated!

The Sears and Roebuck *Wishbook* arrived just once a year and was eagerly anticipated for its pages of new things, clothes, toys, tools and all sort of useful objects and ideas. You could even buy a kit to build a house. In 1937 at the height of the Great Depression the original catalogue store originated in nearby Redwood Falls, just forty miles south of the Molenaar farm. The Sears and Roebuck Christmas Catalogue was appropriately named, full of things that you could wish for, but likely could not afford. The boy, my father, drew a careful circle and placed a marker between the pages denoting his wish. Nordic Skis made of the highest quality quarter sawn ash, nearly eight feet long. No doubt in his eyes, they were perfect in both form and function.

My grandfather passed away in the spring of 1937, on a train platform in South Dakota where he was on a trip intending to buy cattle. He had recently moved his family from the town of Renville to a new home and life as a farmer in Southern Kandiyohi County. For my father, at age thirteen, his mother's words still rang in his ears as his father's coffin was lowered. Her hand was on his shoulder, as she placed a heavy burden there, "you are the man of the family now." By the early winter, I am certain that my father realized the immensity of responsibility for his mother, three younger brothers and sister: the daunting task of farming their acreage and caring for the livestock. I can imagine that my father carefully chose his words as he made his request for the skis. It likely was made by candlelight as this was well before rural electrification came to the farm. "Mother, with these skis I can maybe get the morning animal chores done and get to school on time. I can cut diagonally across the field to the schoolhouse, instead of walking the section road."
My research indicates that twelve dollars was the required amount to buy a pair of '*Wishbook*' Skis in 1937. The family history does not show where the money came from, or even how the decision was reached. It took many years before I was able to consider the significance of this purchase. Literally it meant a little over one mile - fifteen minutes by ski,

versus forty minutes - almost two miles walking via road, to arrive at the District 99 Schoolhouse. Arriving at school in style would also invoke a strong emotion of accomplishment that my father carried with him through his life.

When I was seventeen, my mother, sister and I received new fiberglass Nordic skis under the Christmas tree. Surprisingly there was no new pair of skis under the tree for my father. When I inquired, he merely stated that he already had a pair that he liked. In any event, I am thankful for this gift. While my initial reaction to the skis was puzzlement *(there is only about 5 feet of fall in the entirety of thirty-two sections of land in Holland Township*) I have taken the art of Nordic skiing into my mind and heart. Enough that I crave a good winter snowfall and a peaceful and exhilarating ski through the woods at Sibley State Park.

Even beyond the enjoyment of the sport, in and of itself, there is a deeper meaning for me. One of my prized heritage possessions is this pair of quarter sawn ash, nearly blemish free Nordic Cross Country skis that I discovered hanging from a nail in a shed at my parent's farm. The technology of the modern fiberglass composite Nordic ski of the 20th century is much advanced over the wood. Yet for sheer imaginative power, I prefer the *'Wishbook'* originals. I have a deep sense of pride in the meaning and feeling of accomplishment that they held for my father. Now they hold even more significance for me. On a clear, cold, nearly windless winter morning, with the sun rising at my back, I can imagine that I am the boy, carrying the responsibilities of a man. My chores are complete, and I have stocked the wood and water supply that my mother will need for the day. The District 99 schoolhouse is visible across the field and is a beacon to guide my path. Brothers, sister, cousins are all in the distance, already walking a brisk pace and bundled against the cold. I reach down and strap on my trusted skis and prepare my mind for the responsibilities that lie ahead. As I glide through an ocean of prairie grass and the interruption of an occasional frozen pothole, I pick up speed. The rhythmic motion becomes effortless, and my body warms to the cold. With each kick and subsequent glide I dream that I am flying, and the weight of the world is lifting from my shoulders. He is thirteen, and once again my father is a boy. As he should be.

Part II

The Next Generation!

The New London Story Show is hosted by Heather Westberg King, curator of the Flyleaf Bookstore in our small village of New London, Minnesota. Each show is offered with a specific topic and writers are encouraged to submit and present a story of seven minutes or less in length. These are my own and I hope you enjoy some of my family adventures.

21 Blizzard!

My parents were heroic in the

Saint Patrick's Day Blizzard, 1965!

The winters of 1964 and 1965 brought many challenges to the wide-open prairies of southern Kandiyohi County. Only 3 days of school were held in the months of January and February due to school cancelations from weather. Wednesday March 17th, 1965 began like any other. Around the kitchen table the weather-related announcements on WCCO radio suggested that yet another winter storm was on its way. My father decided that he needed to go to Willmar Implement and bring home our 720 John Deere tractor which had been in the shop for repairs. I was home from kindergarten that morning due to a flu bug, so my mother made a bed for me in the back of our Chevrolet station wagon.

The John Deere dealership was located on the western edge of Willmar adjacent to the airport. The highway headed directly west along the edge of the runway in a Southwesterly direction. The tractor drive to our farm would take about two hours as the top speed was only fourteen miles per hour. My father was bundled up and heading southwest with mom and I following in the car. After about two miles of travel I witnessed a sight that I have never experienced again. People describe the phenomenon as a wall cloud. What I saw that day was a wall blizzard. The sky to the west was completely black as if a curtain had been drawn across it. After a brief roadside consultation with my mother, dad turned the tractor around to return to the JD dealership. He realized that there was no way that he would reach home before the storm struck.

With WCCO radio blaring in the car we heard the announcement that the Roseland School would close early, and children would be sent home on the bus. In the days before cell phones communication was not as instant as today. In a panic from the implement dealer's office my dad called the Roseland School and asked that they not send my sister home so that we could pick her up directly from the school. The trip from Willmar to Roseland was not an easy one with very limited visibility due to whiteout conditions. There was an obvious sense of relief as we reached the schoolhouse. Relief was replaced with panic when my parents discovered that MaryBeth had been sent home on the bus.

With a renewed sense of urgency my father headed our Chevrolet west on a major road, state highway 7. One mile west we made a turn to the south on what we called the "North Road." With even less visibility now, we managed to creep along for another mile. We turned right at DeRuyter's corner and headed west for the last ¾ of a mile to our farm driveway. That is when the full fury of the storm arrived. There was no visibility from within the car. I remember my dad pulling on his heavy coat, winter hat, wrapping in a scarf around his neck and exiting the car after telling my mother to follow him. He walked and Mom followed even though she could barely see him. We inched our way west straight into the wind. There is a slight hill heading west and when we reached the flat on top near our neighbors the Stryker's driveway the visibility got even worse. Mom, losing sight of dad drove into the ditch and was stuck in the deep snow. My dad who I now believed to be a super hero, lifted and pushed the car back onto the roadway. From my bed in the back I clearly recall my mother rolling her window down. Dad stuck his head in the window and stated with the obvious tenor of panic and adrenaline, "Harriet, I don't care where you think the road is, you follow me!" My mother left the window open and leaned out into the wind in order to see more clearly. Once again following my hero dad as we crept to the west. Near the end of our driveway a large snowdrift ended our car trip. We walked the final quarter mile. I was having difficulty staying upright with the gale force wind. My father took my hand, and I was like a kite on a string. We finally reached the shelter of our farmstead grove and safety of our home.

Once we were out of the wind, we could see that a tractor had slid off the road and was stuck in a snowbank. Turns out that was my uncle Vernon trying to head back to his farmstead. The car of our hired hand Dick Raske was also on the yard meaning he was also stranded. There was no Mary

Beth. The bus had turned around and brought the children back to the schoolhouse. I can imagine the plight of the two young teachers with maybe fifteen children stuck in a two-room schoolhouse. Resourcefully they removed the curtains from the large windows and put one down on the floor – directed the children to lay down on top of it and spread the second large curtain over the top. The school had a kitchen, so they had food, but little else to entertain a group of children for the two nights and three days that they were stranded. Eventually a phone call revealed that MaryBeth was safe, and my parents could relax. We lost our electricity, but we had a great time playing games, eating popcorn, and putting together a puzzle by candlelight. Days later when the storm decreased in ferocity my uncle returned to his farmstead and we were able to pick MaryBeth up from the school. After three days when the storm subsided, we were amazed by the drifts of snow. It would have been possible to reach the electrical lines along our driveway from the top of the snowbanks. Many roads had essentially become one-way tunnels with no visibility to the side and limited to the front. My father hired a bulldozer to push the snow out of our livestock pens, yard and push the snow back from our driveway.

There were about two more weeks of winter before the weather improved and the spring melt began. As the spring melt began the immense amount of water in the snowpack was held back into our farmstead. The water was reaching an alarmingly high level to our well. Dad hired a bulldozer to push a channel through the snow on the southwest corner of our farmstead. It was an immense river of water rushing out onto the fields. When my father saw that ice blocks had once again clogged the channel, he drove the model 720JD tractor (with me standing safely between his legs) into the channel to push the ice blocks to the side. With the water nearly reaching our feet on the tractor platform we made multiple passes back and forth until the ice blocks were cleared, and our lake had subsided. I will never forget the storm of a lifetime, the 1965 Saint Patrick's Day blizzard!

22 Dig For Gold!

The KWLM Radio and Olivia Corn Days promotion gave me a chance to dig for a golden prize in a bottle!

My day started ordinarily enough, with me on the couch in my pajamas watching *Bugs Bunny* and his hijinks on a black and white TV. I had already consumed not just one, but two bowls of *Lucky Charms Cereal* and was considering a third. A recent fifth grade report card that suggested I showed potential but had a strong tendency to daydream, and it was on my mind. Daydream! I was pondering why she would write such a thing... When I looked up only a few minutes later *Bugs* was gone, and it now seemed to be mid-episode through a *Pink Panther* cartoon. My mother's slightly hurried voice broke through my reverie. "Put on some clothes, get the shovel out of the shed, your father is busy, your sister is not willing, get in the car, you are coming with me!" I spluttered, "It's Saturday... do I have too... My objections fell upon deaf ears. In the car my mother handed me a letter from the KWLM radio personality none other than Jack Lynch. We did not have a lot of celebrities in Kandiyohi County in 1970, but if there was one, it was Jack on the airwaves of our kitchen radio. As I read, it was as if his baritone monologue was in the car with me...

Congratulations ... Your name was picked by one of the sponsors on our Gold Diggers promotion. This entitles you to join us this Saturday, October 3rd, for the big dig-in. The place is at the site of the national corn husking contest, at Olivia. There will be 16 capsules buried... one worth $1500 and the other 15 worth $100 apiece. If you do not feel up to digging... you will be permitted to substitute someone for yourself. We wish you luck. Jack Lynch, KWLM

So I was to be the substitute. This revelation did nothing to improve my mood. Standing before a wooden speaker's platform in Olivia, my frame of mind sank even lower as I realized what was about to happen. Various dignitaries were welcomed from mayor to corn husker, and everyone in between. Each had a very important and lengthy message to share. My Saturday was a shambles! Delivered via helicopter, former Senator and Vice President of the United States Hubert Horatio Humphrey was the final speaker of the morning. Mr. Humphrey proved to be a great orator, he was a bit lengthy, but he was a Minnesotan and we loved him! My considerations were interrupted by Jack Lynch directing all *Gold Diggers* to find their way to a position in the one-acre field immediately behind us. The acre was plowed black, encircled with a fence and an entry gate. The field seemed impossibly large, but the crowd was bigger. Men and women dressed from Sunday best to traditional work clothes pushed forward to find places in the field. Amid the chaotic rush of people to find positions, I found a nice spot right inside the gate. As others fought for the best locations all across the field, I reassured myself on this negative logic, "Why walk all the way to the far side of the field, when I can stay right here and find nothing just as easily?" I must have spoken my thoughts aloud as a friendly flannelled shirted man suggested that this was likely a lost cause, and we were wasting our time. But in true Minnesota fashion we both agreed that it was a nice day to be outside and things could be worse. You bet!

A pistol shot rang out and we began frantically digging. Shovels, rakes and tools of all manner were moving dirt at a rapid pace and the sounds of exertion were in the air. It was utter chaos! I struck a rock with my shovel. "Better move over a bit," I thought. The flannel shirt man caught my attention and said, "Hey, I think you have something there." The rock was something. The something was a white bottle in the dirt. I fell to my hands and knees and pulled it up. The same man suggested that my mother and I take the bottle up to the speaker's platform. Jack Lynch opened our capsule and revealed, "Congratulations, you are the grand prize winner of fifteen hundred dollars!"

It took some time for all sixteen bottles to be found, but found they were, and the winners were gathered to chairs on the platform. Vice President Humphrey stepped forward to congratulate the winner and incorrectly shook the hand...of the man sitting next to me. In his strong voice he commended the person's luck and good fortune on winning the grand prize. "Come visit me in the capital and let's get better acquainted," he

offered. I was stunned and disappointed. "How could this vice-presidential case of mistaken identity happen? How could another man take credit for my accomplishment? He was merely a one-hundred-dollar winner." It seemed cruel and unfair. It was a dirty rotten trick. It was injustice! "What if Vice President Humphrey had correctly recognized me as the winner? What if I had gone on to Washington D.C. to be Mr. Humphrey's right-hand advisor? I, Jimmy Molenaar, trusted consultant on breakfast cereals, school recess and television cartoons! What if! What if?"
As my mother and I came home the evening of the dig, with lights flashing and horn blaring, my father greeted us with a mischievous grin. He was aware of our good fortune as he had heard mom being interviewed on the radio. Numerous car salesmen had already called to the farm with *once in a lifetime deals* on automobiles. Perhaps Dad suggested, "The next time you win a prize it might be better not to announce to the radio world that you will use the money to buy a different car." Then he laughed and gave us both a big hug.

Now, almost fifty years later, I have a much more positive memory about my *Dig for Gold* experience. Enough that I can daydream about a Saturday morning spent in my pajamas, including a trip to a store to buy a box of *Lucky Charms* cereal. I might briefly consider buying a lottery ticket. Probably not, I had already won once and why push my luck? Mostly I just think about that time with my mother on a long-ago Saturday. We were a team, we dug for gold, and we had struck the mother lode. Fifteen hundred dollars may not seem like much today, but it was enough then to buy a used lemon yellow 1967 Chevrolet station wagon, complete with a third-row rear seat! I fondly recall the family camping trips, travel adventures and misadventures we had in that car. Lemon, probably not the best color for a used vehicle. But then again, in my mind's eye that car is no longer yellow, but has now faded to a deeper, richer, shade of gold.

23 Bears and Border Insecurity

“Harry, the bears are coming your way!” Mrs. Smith added her voice and additional drama to the adventure.

If there was a way to measure excitement, my imaginary *'Adventure Meter'* needle for my mother and grandmother Esther pointed far to the low side; my sister Mary Beth and father were in the middle; and my own arrow pointed to high and ready for excitement. My father often suggested that we had an adventure gene in our blood and thus we were pre-destined to camp. When I was six or seven these forces came together in a remarkable escapade involving the wilderness.

In 1965 *The Sawbill Trail* was not much more than a glorified logging road. The road turned hard left from Tofte on Lake Superior and featured roller coaster like climbs, drops and sharp curves. An occasional passing logging truck created an explosion of dust and depending on your perspective it was cause for panic or pleasure. It was well into the evening when we arrived to the aroma of pine trees at campsite number two, Sawbill Lake Campground of the soon to be formed Boundary Waters Canoe Area Wilderness.

"This is the wilderness!" So stated Mrs. Smith, our neighbor and resident of campsite number one. Campsite one also appeared to be occupied by a shiny new silver Airstream camper and a seemingly more introverted Mr. Smith and their young daughter. Mrs. Smith continued, "If I were you, I would turn right around and head back to civilization. I would never camp here with young children in a flimsy tent." Then with some fanfare she concluded in a much more authoritarian voice, "There are bears in this campground!"

When Mrs. Smith realized that we were not 'turning around' she invited us into her Airstream for grilled cheese sandwiches and soup. Her camper was so shiny and new, unlike anything I had experienced before or possibly since. She explained her hospitality, "I just could not imagine you poor folks having to set up camp and cook supper in the dark." As we were leaving the camper Mrs. Smith suggested to my father in a low conspiratorial voice, "Harry, if the bears come into the campground, I'll shine my spotlight on them and give you a warning."

My father built a campfire – directly in front of our tent entrance to supposedly scare off bears, or at least to appease my mother and grandma that he was doing something about the situation. On the other hand, the potential for excitement seemed to be shaping up nicely for me as I snuggled into my sleeping bag and drifted off to sleep.

Sometime later that evening I woke up from the sound of a kettle being clanged with a wooden spoon. Mrs. Smith was shouting, “Harry, the bears! HARRY! THE BEARS ARE COMING YOUR WAY!” Mr. Smith was playing the spotlight beam across our tent wall, and there was more kettle banging and shouting. My father was outside the tent. It seemed my chance for real adventure was imminent and I got up to join him. I had never seen a live bear, and this seemed like the perfect opportunity! Then my mother firmly stated, “You get right back in your sleeping bag young man!”

The following day we learned that black bears had come into the campground to knock over garbage cans seeking an easy meal. From the appearance of sleepless eyes, disheveled hair, and adult overall grumpiness, I just knew that we would not be spending another night at Sawbill Lake. This would prove to be one of the great disappointments of my life.

Adventure genetics are hard to deny. Approximately one year later and in the following summer my parents loaded the car, and we headed north for a new camping adventure. For this trip we were accompanied in the back seat by my somewhat adventurous and gregarious Great Aunt Anna. Anna was known for her ability to make Red-Hot Anise Hard Rock Candy which she would randomly distribute to my sister and me. She would then whisper, “don’t tell your parents, this is our secret.” Of course there was really no possibility of stealth as the candy had an aroma so strong it could clean out your nostrils and maybe your companion’s sinuses as well. If you bit into it, I swear it could strip the enamel from your teeth.

As our station wagon rolled to a stop at the daunting structure of the Grand Portage International Border Crossing and newly constructed bridge across the Pigeon River into Canada, the imposing figure of an immaculately uniformed customs officer approached our car and asked, “where do you intend to travel?” My father replied, “The circle route through Ontario and around Lake Superior.” The officer then asked, “Do you have any alcohol, tobacco, illegal drugs or firearms?” My father responded carefully “NO”, “NO”, “NO”. Then after a pause, a firm but cautious “YES” was uttered.

Suddenly my dormant *'Adventure Meter'* was activated to high alert. The air seemed to escape from the car as everyone took a deep breath and considered what would happen next. Would this be the end of our vacation? Would we be turning back? Was I destined for even greater disappointment? Anna began passing out rock candy in an attempt to calm our shaken nerves. The aroma of Red-Hot tension was overwhelmingly filling our car.

The officer slightly raised his hat and mirrored sunglasses, wiped his brow, and he carefully peered at my father. "It is illegal to allow firearms to cross the border." My father nodded the affirmative but then responded in a low voice. "Well officer, last year we were camping not too far from here and the bears... well, - my wife believes that bears do not respect the border, so she insisted that the only way she would go on a camping trip to Canada, is with a gun for protection... I have a twelve-gauge Remington Wing-Master shotgun in the back, under the tent."

As I reflect back, I wonder if the officer was a father, a husband or maybe just a compassionate public servant. He seemed to be having an internal argument. Drops of water appeared on his forehead. After a time, he shrugged, wiped the sweat from his brow, and suggested that we ***drive on***. With a tip of the hat, a wink, and a slight smile, he left us with these parting words. "Leave the gun in the car, with the aroma of that rock candy, I think don't think the bears of Canada will come near you!"

Each person in this story has a special place in my heart as I consider their personality and my heart swells with the memory. On the Ontario shore of Lake Superior is a long steep downward sloping grade in the highway, possibly several miles, which creates the illusion that at the end your car will plunge into the deep blue cold of the waters of the Big Lake. Perhaps the moment was triggered from the confidence of telling the truth in front of his children, maybe it was the pride of passing a test in a moment of insecurity, or it was just a surge of the adventure gene that caused my father to press the "gas pedal" full to the floor. The resulting momentary surge towards oblivion created an apostrophe mark of reaction across the adventure spectrum. With that action, my father had clearly surpassed anything that I could have imagined.

24 Livestock Exchange

The Livestock Exchange "castle" had a kiosk with a greater variety and quantity of candy than I could imagine!

We were livestock farmers and cared for our animals. Making sure that every animal had fresh water and feed was a twenty-four hour, three hundred and sixty-five day a year responsibility. Taking a day off from animal care was never an option. Our cattle needed to be fed twice a day. This meant climbing up a dusty silo chute ladder and adjusting the machinery to bring the silage down. Pig feed was corn ground with soybean protein, and was a full day, once-a-week task. We baled alfalfa hay in the summer and also harvested oat straw to provide clean dry bedding for all the animals. Most of the crops raised on our farm were for the purpose of feeding animals. The lessons I learned and the knowledge I gained remain with me to this day. I am often offended by people who think that animal agriculture is cruelty. This was not the way of our farm.

It all started with Max the piglet. My father would buy young pigs and raise them up to market weight and subsequent sale. On one particular trip MaryBeth and I rode along in our pickup truck. I would have been about five years old and MaryBeth eight. The farmer had two piglets that were too small to sell and so he gave them to us. I don't remember the name my sister chose but my black pig with a white belt (Hampshire breed) was named Max. Some time went by, and Max grew larger under my father's care. One day dad took me over to a geometric shaped pig house on wooden skids which was called an 'A' house. In the one animal sized shelter was Max and seven baby piglets. I fairly flew up to the house to announce to my grandmother Ivel, mom and sister that "Max had babies! Max has seven baby piglets!" My grandmother Ivel smiled and said, "I think Max will need a new name. Why don't you call her Maxine?" So from then on she was known as Maxine, but I still called her Max for short!

The next venture I recall was when I was a bit older, our 4-H club motivated me to enroll in the beef business. My mother's cousins, the Strand Brothers, were well known for their Polled Herefords (polled means no horns naturally). The expectation for a Polled Hereford was red with a white face. When a couple of calves showed up with black markings, they were culled from the Strand herd and became my project calves. I don't think they were given names so I will just call them Red and Black. It was a good amount of work caring for them. We trudged across the yard every day sometimes in knee deep snow or foot gripping mud carrying equal weights of water in one hand and grain in the other. We practiced teaching the calves to lead with a rope around their neck. The bigger of the two calves (Red), was tame and trained well, but the smaller (Black), had a not only had a black marking across his shoulders, but he also had a dark streak in his heart. He was a renegade. When the county fair came along my dad surprised me with the announcement that MaryBeth would show Red. Because I was a boy, I would lead the wilder Black. We had borrowed show halters from the DeRuyter family to save money. Since we had no experience showing a calf, Valerie Strand niece of the Strand brothers, helped us wash and groom them for showing. When the time came, we led our calves into the show ring, and walked them in a circle while the judge observed the animals. When we lined up the judge began arranging us in order top to bottom. Being designated to last place was not my primary concern because my rowdy Black pulled hard enough that he broke the halter, and I wrapped my arms around his neck desperately hoping to maintain control. I would not have been more embarrassed if I had been standing in the ring naked. I tried to avoid the judge's gaze but no such luck as he came over and handed me a rope loop. He gave me a sympathetic pat and a knowing glance before moving on. I survived the experience with a white participation ribbon while my sister received a red. Valerie Strand earned a purple ribbon and a trip to the MN State Fair. Our calves were brought home and returned to their barn. When it was time for Red and Black to be sold, Blackie escaped by jumping through a barn window taking a good portion of the old barn wall with him. He began running and could not be approached as he would charge anyone trying to come near him. Black's run covered almost twelve miles. He was unapproachable and out of control. We borrowed a tranquilizer gun which mercifully subdued Black, but he was never the same. I was crushed from this experience. The lessons of farm life and animal death are not always easy. I do think that they prepared me for many of life's challenges yet to come.

I decided that showing animals was not for me. I focused on food production and making money. At any one time throughout high school and college I had about twelve beef animals and over one hundred pigs being fed. I even constructed my own barn to house sixty pigs. During this time I did not name my animals, but always gave them good care. I recall several blazing hot summer days where my dad and I would construct water misting systems to keep our animals cool. We always made sure they had plenty of bedding and fresh water. During winter blizzards, many times we were unable to see twenty feet much less drive across our farmyard. We used a toboggan sled to pull straw bedding and feed over and around high snowbanks to care for our animals.

I loved my animals but (with the exception of Max) naming them gave them a connotation that they were pets. They had a purpose and I believe that reason is to provide healthy nutritious food to people. Hence the livestock exchange. When our animals were ready to become food, they were shipped to the market at South Saint Paul. Buyers would meet with a seller from Central Livestock who would represent us in the transaction. Almost always we would arise early in the morning and drive to South Saint Paul to see that our animals were given fresh water, food, and adequate bedding. Following the transaction, we made our way to the Exchange Building on Concord Avenue. It was there that we went up a flight of stairs to be greeted by a kiosk of all manner of tobacco products but more importantly to me an array of candy such as I have never seen before or since. Every flavor of life saver roll was on display. More candy bars than I could imagine. My dad always let me purchase a couple of treats. We then went up a curving cast iron staircase and made our way to the offices of Central Livestock where we could pick up our check of proceeds from the sale. Through a window we could watch Lyle Landphere announce the noon-time markets broadcast across the Midwest on just about every radio station. If I stood on the couch in the lobby, I could watch the whole show and I was just about nose to nose through the glass to Mr. Landphere.

Central Livestock was a cooperative venture where the farmers owned the business and shared in the profits or losses. My family had a long history with Central as my grandfather served as the Central shipping association manager in Renville. We continued this relationship, as my father sold all his animals through Central. When a board of directors' member was needed from our area my father was elected. He served a number of years on the board where he described himself as representing the farmers' best interests. Some on the board seemed to be more interested in the status of the position. In any case eventually my father was elected to chairman of the board. He became a highly respected leader in the farm community. His desire was for farmers of all operation sizes, small or large, to be treated fairly in the marketplace. While I was farming all of my animals were sold through Central and I have fond memories communicating with the men of Central. I was even asked to serve as a voting member to the annual meeting representing the Roseland Shipping Association. Even though I was still a boy those experiences allowed me to be very proud of my father. He only had an eighth-grade education and yet he stood tall among some of the largest and well-educated farmers of the Midwest.

25 Two Tents!

Many nights spent in an adventure made of canvas!

A man was having trouble sleeping so the doctor sent him home with the following instructions. "The next time you wake up write down what you were dreaming about and report what happened." After two nights the man met with his doctor and explained that he had awoken in a cold sweat both times. The doctor asked him, "what was your dream?" The man responded, "I dreamed I was in the middle of the forest, and I was an 'A'-frame pup tent with a bunch of mis-behaving boy scouts." "Aha!" said the doctor, "that is very interesting. What happened the second night?" The man replied, "The second night I dreamed that I was a half dome with fiberglass poles and a rainfly. The occupants were a bunch of senior citizens, the roof was leaking, and the adults were snoring loud enough to shake my poles." "Aha!" said the doctor, "I know exactly what is wrong with you." "What, asked the man?" The doctor replied, by stating, "It is my professional opinion that you are two tents!" ie. 'too tense' (If my children are reading this they will groan as it is one of my favorite bad dad jokes)

After visiting the Minnesota State Fair in 1967 my parents visited the big box store of the day – the Sears multi story shopping building at the corner of Snelling Avenue and University in St. Paul to buy my sister and I school clothes. Sears had a room on the first level of the store where my father spotted a canvas tent set up on display that would sleep eight people. We were all in the car when he returned with excitement in his voice, "I offered them fifty dollars for the display tent, and they accepted." He was so excited and pleased. I truly believed that my father imagined the adventures and experiences it would provide for our family. We used it to sleep in the backyard on sweltering summer nights. We camped at Sawbill Lake, all of the parks on the north shore of Lake Superior, and we even made a circle route trip around the largest of the great lakes returning through Michigan and Wisconsin. When our cousins Lois and Paul invited us to join them on a trip to Estes Park Colorado, we joined in. It was an amazing experience that I will never forget. A mountain snowfall in mid-August left our tent damp enough that mold developed in our storage cabinet over the winter. The mold spots developed into holes large enough to allow rainwater into my father's beloved tent. No amount of patching seemed to fix the problem. He tried covering the tent with plastic which worked with mixed results. Somehow our tent seemed to attract massive rainstorms of which the layer of plastic captured and usually collapsed one end or both of our quarters. On one memorable occasion we watched from the car while my father attempted to pull the plastic to release the water that had puddled on the roof. He was successful as the cold water came off of the tent but frigidly ran down my dad's neck. Still, he was cheerful and made arrangements to visit a laundromat to dry our belongings and then spend the night in a small but dry north-shore cabin.

When I was a senior in college some friends and I decided to go on a camping trip. Steve, Jack, Brad, and Kent scratched together what we had, and I provided the tent. We ended up at a small-town park in Paynesville just behind a gas station. When I asked if I could borrow the tent my father agreed but gave a warning, there is a piece of plastic in the shed. You better take that along as the tent is leaky and it looks like rain. All in all, we had a good plan and everything we needed. The first day we went fishing on Lake Koronis from shore. Kent was inexperienced and had never been fishing in his life. We explained what to do and sent him off to cast thinking 'not a chance.' That was the case for us upperclassmen, but when Kent came back running and shouting "I caught one! I caught a fish" we were astounded to note he had indeed caught a beautiful Bass. Unfortunately, it was two weeks before the bass season opener. Steve and I bumped fists and said, "let's let Jack tell him he has to put it back." The next day we rented a nine-foot boat and attached a massive old ten horse Johnson fishing motor that belonged to Jack's dad. The nine-foot boat would have been right sized for two guys of our stature, but the five of us lowered the boat to within one inch of the water line. When Jack opened the throttle on the engine the front of our dingy was taking a nosedive with water rushing over the bow. Steve shouted, “I can’t swim” and Jack shut the engine down. After that we did a one mile per hour put-put out to our fishing spot. An hour later when we finally settled on a spot to fish Brad announced, “I have to pee, take me back to shore.” The rest of us said, “pee over the side, we are not going back!” When Brad attempted this maneuver, we rocked the boat enough that he had trouble maintaining his balance. Steve then put his hand in the water splashing and commenting, “wow the water is so nice and cool today. Doesn’t it sound nice the splashing in the water?” After much laughter at poor Brad’s expense, we relented and took the boat back to shore ending our fishing adventure. Back to the camp. It was surprisingly hot and humid for a day in May, and it looked like it might rain, so I covered the tent with the plastic. My covering came as close to creating a sauna tent as anything without a fire could achieve. We then discovered that the piece of plastic that my father provided had been used to cover the previous year’s corn silage pile. The aroma was very overpowering, and the heat of day caused it to permeate the tent sleeping quarters. A slightly cooler evening did nothing to alleviate the stench of old corn silage. Steve bailed out to sleep in the back of his pickup truck while the rest of us did our best to not asphyxiate.

I have used many tents with more modern materials and that are a great deal lighter in weight than my father’s massive canvas job. But none rival the memories and laughter that I experience when I think back to the Sears discount model that gave my father and our family so much adventure. I believe that part of the fun of camping is overcoming the disasters and the bonding that occurs when things go wrong. So today when my friends want to tease me, they will chide, “Hey Jim, you want to go camping? Still got a piece of silage plastic to put on the tent?” I usually respond with a mumbling non-descript response like, “no thank you. I’m just a bit ‘too tense’ for a tenting trip right now!”

26 Good Men!

We were good men! The fall corn harvest

was my favorite time of the year.

I can still recall the day that George Dykema came to work for my dad and uncle. My best guess was that I was in 3rd grade and the year was probably 1967. The summer and fall had been challenging. High rainfall had left the fields wet and soggy with many areas of standing water. Saturday morning broke cool gray and cloudy, which was typical for that year. I clearly recall having a morning meeting at Vernon's kitchen table and I listened with rapt attention at the conversation.

Apparently, a new hired man would be coming to pick corn for a day as a sort of trial period for considering employment. Vern and dad were concerned that he would be frustrated with the wet fields and that maybe he might not want to come back the following day. Earlier that fall we had purchased a good used 730 diesel John Deere tractor to use for plowing. An agreement was reached to attach the 730 to the New Idea corn picker for the day – even though that was not the original plan. Let's see how it goes for a few days they figured. At noon that day I met George for the first time. At age 65 he had recently retired from his own farm. As he came in the door to the kitchen, I can remember his cheerful greeting. The 730 and the New Idea picker suited his taste, and he confirmed this by saying "that's my tractor" a phrase that was often repeated over the fourteen years that George was a part of our farm. George was hired and his only stipulation was that his name was on the 730 tractor, and it remained so for the entire time that he worked at our farm.

For much of that fall – a second tractor and 200-foot-long cable were rigged to attach a second tractor on dry ground, employed to pull the 730 and corn picker through the standing water and mud. It was my job to drive the second tractor. Even with these challenges I remember a new sense of enthusiasm and positive attitude around the farm that was brought by George and his personality.

Corn picking was always a special time on the farm, I think George's favorite. When I was home from school it was my job to haul wagons to and from the field. I would park the empty at the end of the field and hold the wagon tongue while George backed the picker to the wagon. I placed the pin and George began another round of harvesting. It was then my task to back up and hook the full wagon to the haul tractor, drive home and empty the wagon and return to the field to repeat the process. George liked the days that I was home as he rarely had to wait for an empty wagon. The inevitable switch was made with a friendly wave and happy greeting. It was a good day when I could keep George rolling and pick almost 20 acres of corn.

Both of my grandfathers had passed away before I was born, so in many ways George filled that role for me. Morning lunch at 10:00am was a favorite of mine since we would gather at the kitchen table, listen to the markets on the radio and discuss issues of the day. One of the first things I began to enjoy about George was his positive attitude, sense of humor and lively sayings of wisdom. I'm sure I have forgotten more of these than I remember. One of my favorites (that I still use) was a favorite following a task well done or hard work completed. "We're good men!" No late-night talk show host ever delivered a punchline with more enthusiasm or timing than George. "Let's chores" or "I'm chore-sing this weekend," announced the times when he took care of the livestock feeding for us. If the request involved a weekend, he would always say "I'll have to review my contract and speak to the union." Of course we all knew that the union was his wonderful wife, Laura. When speaking of money – he suggested "remember Jimmy, it's not what you make but what you save that counts!" or "When I was your age, I pitched manure for a full day and earned 25cents. Just think of it, a quarter for a day of hard work!" I can't recall George getting upset or using foul language. When frustrated he might say "that's the bunk" or "that's just terrible – terrible." Mostly I just remember a cheerful attitude as a positive role model to me.

I learned quite a bit about employer – employee relationships by observing my father and George in action. I recall my dad saying that what he appreciated about George was how he "made our farm his own." Apparently, some previous farm hands would do only the task they were told to do and nothing more. Dad always felt that George treated the equipment, livestock, crops and farm as if they were his own. He looked out for the best interests of our farm and family. I know that dad always asked George for advice on decisions such as selling livestock or crops, when to plant, harvest etc. George was willing to give advice and input but respected my father as the decision maker. For the most part I believe my father listened to George and he became a trusted advisor in the farming operation. I can't ever recall George and dad sharing a cross word or ever having a disagreement. Having someone he trusted allowed our family to take an occasional vacation away from the farm and know that things were in good hands.

There were many things that George was willing to do for my dad and only a few jobs that were off limits. When mom went back to fulltime work, I think dad wanted to try and help out with household tasks as much as possible. I came home from school one rainy day to find that dad and George had spent the day washing walls in the house. Together they cleaned windows, cooked meals and I think maybe vacuumed too. Apparently when George returned home, he offered to his wife Laura that he would help her out – now realizing how tough those jobs were. "That's hard work!" he stated.

We bought a Bobcat loader in the fall of 1978, and I was the first to operate the new machine. After lifting the first bucket of runny hog manure high – and having most of it spill on my lap, I learned that you need to level the bucket as you raise it up. George had seen enough. After some good-natured laughter, he announced that the Bobcat was a piece of equipment that he did not intend to operate. To the best of my knowledge he never did.

Painting was not on George's list. Even though his brother Johnny was a well-known and respected painter in the area, George did not like painting. When asked he politely declined by saying, "I never found a brush that fit my hand." To the best of my knowledge, he did no painting over the fourteen years at our farm with one notable exception. In the fall of 1982 after my father passed away in a farm accident. George was the glue that really held our family together. His labor and emotional support were so needed in that time. When George suggested that our small garage really could use a coat of fresh red paint, I took his advice, got the needed supplies, and started in on the job. I was very 'blue' over the loss of my father and painting gave me time to mourn and think about my family's altered future. I still get tears in my eyes when I remember George driving up on the yard, getting out of his car and announcing, "I found a paint brush that fits my hand – where do you want me to start?" It was a gesture that only a grandfather would make.

I had been contemplating leaving my teaching job in St. Peter to return home and take over the farm. It was while we were painting that George gave me some wise advice. "Jimmy, there was no better man than your father. Look how he struggled to make ends meet and keep this farm going. Stay with your teaching job." In the following years George would remind me. "I'm so glad you're not farming – Aren't you glad you're not farming Jimmy? Times are so tough, look at the prices, it's terrible-just terrible!" Mom used to remind me that I used to say to my dad "It wouldn't be much fun farming without George, would it?" I think that sums it up. Together we were Good Men. I am so thankful that he was part of my life!

Written as a eulogy for George, April 18, 2002

27 People to People Goodwill

I was a farm boy in Red Square, Moscow!

My agriculture and FFA instructor Mr. Glen Christiansen was probably the biggest influence in my young life besides my parents. When he introduced the idea of an international FFA trip to Europe, I took interest. My friend Dan Lippert had participated in the FFA Goodwill trip the previous year. The stories he told of this adventure were intriguing enough that three of my friends Steve, Tom, Bruce, and I along with twenty-seven other FFA members from around Minnesota signed up. The all-inclusive trip cost about three thousand dollars which was a large amount for me. I had made enough money raising my own pigs and cattle that I wrote out a check for the full amount. I remember a classmate who opted out of the experience and instead bought a hot car. I remember Mr. Christiansen commenting that the auto would be rusted out and in a junkyard in a few years, but that we would have the education and experience of our trip for a lifetime.

We had a two-hour orientation session at the Minnesota FFA convention in April but little other preparation for the experience. Mr. Christiansen directed us to order an FFA jacket that had an inner zipper pocket where we could store our passport and travelers' checks. I had flown once from Arizona to home but many of the FFA members had never been on a plane, much less travel abroad. In 1976 there were no check points in the airport. All members of our family and those of the other FFA members walked with us to the boarding gate and gave hugs goodbye as we boarded our jet. My mother later recounted that she expressed a real feeling of regret to my father as they watched us taxi down the runway. "Did we do the right thing in allowing him to go?"

The FFA Goodwill trip allowed us to view farms and life in England, Denmark, Poland, the Soviet Union, Switzerland, and the Netherlands. My Aunt and Godmother Gretchen presented me with a journal book and suggested that I write a bit about each day's activity so that I could remember my experience. I was determined to have a souvenir from each country and was fortunate to do so. My mother's creativity put all of those artifacts into a 'memory box' which hangs above my desk. Not too long ago I discovered an old cardboard box with an itinerary and many of the flyers and memories of this experience. Digging through the dusty papers and photo slides I took a trip back in time.

At New York's JFK Airport we moved out of our comfort zone by the 'Moonies' or zealots dressed in white robes with shaved heads and were apparently hanging out to promote their cause. As rural farm kids we were shocked to be exposed to this type of public display. We embarked for an even longer overnight flight to London's Heathrow airport arriving at dawn. This was followed by a two-hour bus ride to our hotel in London. We were told to report to the dining room of our residence at 10am. When about half of our group was tardy to the breakfast (understandably so I think) we were dressed down by the host-waiter. He called us childish, rude, irresponsible, ugly young American's and that such behavior was not acceptable. We should grow up. Of course those of us at the tables resented that we were present for the tongue lashing – while the others were blissfully sleeping. The farms were bright green from their grassland pastures with most of the farms appearing to be livestock oriented. Souvenir acquired: two miniature guard dolls a replica of the royal guard at Buckingham Palace.

Denmark: The best porkchop I have ever eaten was in a thatched roof pub in the countryside. We were surprised to find bottles of beer and hard alcohol on the table with no age limit to partake. I had no experience and tried a few sips while others imbibed liberally. We observed a Hans Christian Anderson statue of a mermaid which graced the entrance of the harbor. An evening visit to Tivoli gardens amusement park rivaled anything we had in the US. I found a pay phone and called home to mom and dad. It was the fourth of July 1976 and I had missed the bicentennial celebration of our country. (also my mom's birthday) I began to feel a bit homesick. Souvenir: A miniature Viking complete with hat horns and a red beard!

Poland: Monuments to soldier heroes of WWII were a grim reminder of the horror. Buildings with damage still evident from the bombing and violence of the war. Polish workers were picketing for a better wage and living conditions. Vodka and whiskey were readily available at every meal including breakfast. My friends and I discussed how much we appreciated our home and freedoms. We toured government owned massive greenhouses of vegetable crops. I couldn't help thinking, "wouldn't it be better if the people owned their own food production?" Souvenir: a wooden replica of a 4000 B.C. Celt of the La Tène culture.

Soviet Union: We flew into Moscow and nervously arrived at customs. Our passports were taken from us to be returned when we left the country. Even more disconcerting was a written form to declare how much money we were carrying into the country. The intent was to put a halt to black marketing. We experienced more alcohol. Vodka and whiskey bottles which adorned the tables in even greater amount than we had previously observed. We experienced *Swan Lake* at the Moscow Ballet in Red Square. People were waiting in what appeared to be a one-half mile long line in order to view Lenin's Tomb. We visited a museum which had on display the ornate carriages of the pre-Soviet Russian Noble Class. A short flight on a very cramped plane took us to Krasnodar which was the heart of Russian agriculture production. Our first stop was a Russian Circus. Very similar to those I had seen at the Met Center in Bloomington MN but still interesting. We visited a collective farm, and we were astonished by the sight of fields that may have been over 30,000 hectares in size. (A hectare is equivalent to 2.5 US acres) A small collective village appeared to have very productive gardens where the people who lived there and worked on the collective, were allowed to grow their own food. My friend Steve tripped and fell against our hotel window breaking the glass. I assured him that people do not get sent to Siberia for breaking window glass. Then in further thought I asked him if they received postcards in the Gulag so that I could send notes to him. Turns out he was able to pay five dollars for the repair and all was well.

Several of our entourage vocally expressed how superior our United States Agriculture System was to the collectives. My friends and I kept those thoughts private even though we agreed. When it was time to leave the Soviet Block, I counted and recounted my money declaration. I had two hundred dollars more than when I entered the country. I had not engaged in selling my belt or blue jeans in the black market as had others in our group. I had done nothing wrong, but I was filled with anxiety as I hid two hundred dollars in my underwear. I made it through customs all the while thinking, Siberia is probably very nice! Souvenir: A 'Pioneer Doll' representing the Russian settlers of centuries past.

Switzerland was a dramatic change as we were bused off to the Swiss Alps. The switchback up the mountain was chilling as the bus front needed to extend past the road (wheels are set farther back) in order to make the turns. We walked through a tunnel that water had carved out of a massive glacier, marveled at Lucerne a city on a beautiful mountain lake. The Swiss cheese plant inspired me to buy a quarter of a wheel block of cheese to give to my father. I was encouraged to keep the block moist, or it would be dry crumbles by the time we returned home. This was a bad idea in retrospect. Souvenir: A small doll of a Swiss mountain man playing a long Alphorn which was used to call the cow's home. Very cool!

A train ride along the Danube River and valley brought us to the Netherlands. It was there that I was introduced to the *Molen* the wind powered mill or water pump that is iconic of Holland and our family's namesake. We toured the city of Amsterdam by boat through their extensive canal system. The *Polder* is the name that the industrious Hollanders have given the drained sea bottom which is used for extensive agriculture food production. After a long bus ride we observed the massive sea dam that keeps the sea water out of the Polder, but as the tide flows out, allows the freshwater rivers and boats/vessels to travel out to reach the ocean. An impressive feat of engineering. We were experiencing some warm temperatures, and my suitcase was conducting a science experiment. Turns out that moist cheese wrapped in a wet towel in a hot bag provided the ideal environment for green mold and a tremendously strong odor. It permeated the upper thirteenth floor of our hotel. Fortunately, I found a dumpster immediately below our balcony and I performed a perfectly aligned drop of the cheese block, towel and odor into the garbage. I was saved from the humiliation of carrying the smell down the elevator and out the lobby.

While in Amsterdam my aunt Gretchen made arrangements for some relatives to contact me at our hotel and invite me to their home. Their abode was narrow, tall with a steep staircase and shared exterior walls with the neighboring homes. It very much reminded me of the architecture of my home on the farm. We had a nice backyard visit about life in America and Holland. They offered cheese, crackers, and sherry. I was not aware of the term sherry, but my host explained that it was another name for wine. No thank you I replied, "We only have wine to celebrate at special events like Christmas." Turns out my cousin was a newspaper columnist for the Amsterdam Times, and he wrote an article *Jim from America*. In his writing he pointed out the strange custom of Jim's family only having alcohol on Christmas eve. When my mother had the article translated by her friend Phyllis, mom was aghast. Not only did she question why I made that statement about wine, but she was literally embarrassed that our translator friend would know that we had a glass of sherry at Christmas. Souvenir: The newspaper article and a doll complete with Dutch girl hat and costume.

When I returned home my mother had the coins, currency and the souvenirs from each country made into a memory box. There is a space for each country and a middle place of honor for the newspaper article. It is a treasured keepsake that hangs above my desk. Mr. Christiansen told us that an outcome of the trip would be a greater appreciation for our life here in America. He was right and I still do!

28 Immature

We were young and immature!

Comedian and bestselling author Dave Barry said it best, "You are only young once, but you can always be immature!" He backs this statement up with several fine examples in his book *Lessons from Lucy.* If anything, this anecdote completely explains my approach to college and my relationships while there. I met Steve the first day of kindergarten and we have been friends ever since that day. Due to a tragic farm accident in the fourth grade, Steve has artificial limbs below both knees. He managed this condition so successfully that most people were not even aware of his situation. We have been together through grade school, high school, athletics, FFA and we even went on a People-to-People Goodwill Tour to Europe and the Soviet Union. I feel fortunate that we both had careers as agriculture educators for over forty years. I am well aware of the triumphs and challenges that my good friend has faced from his accident. At the University of Minnesota we shared a small dormitory room in Baily hall right above a small parking lot. When our friends Jack and Susan returned and 'parked' for a time in that area, Steve brought out his high-powered flashlight. He would do a quick downward flash out our dorm window and through the windshield to illuminate the front seat of Jack's Dodge Dart car revealing any activities that Jack and Susan may have been conducting. Jack mildly confronted us for our behavior, but it only encouraged our immaturity.

Steve, Jack and I were enrolled in the same home horticulture lecture class. One day we were late and there was no way to gracefully enter the theatre style hall other than to walk across the front of the room in front of the entire class. We were doing our best to stay under the radar of Professor Mullen when Steve's left foot broke off and he tumbled to the floor. He sat up holding his foot in his hand. The co-eds who lined the front row directly in front of us were gasping and fainting from this action. Jack and I were doubled up in laughter as Steve tried to explain with little effect "This is not what you think, it's not real." Which only caused a more panicked response from the audience. We made an awkward but successful exit as Jack and I each took a shoulder to help him up and out. We walked Steve back to our dorm room minus one left foot. After a visit to the limb company Steve returned with new legs and was now several inches taller. "I decided that the length of my wingspan called for a bit more height" he suggested. Those of us in the know got many chuckles as people looked at him with a funny glance. Something was different from the last time they saw him, but they were not quite sure what it was.

The St. Paul Campus intramural *Water Buffalo basketball team* only allowed members who were over 200 pounds or had never played organized basketball. Jack and Mark 'Sheepdog' Pearson were our point guards. They were spelled by a fairly athletic wrestler Dean Kaehler, who was no better with a ball than the rest of us. On one memorable night Jack received the ball on the opening tip and drove to the basket. He was oblivious to our shouts that he was shooting and missing the opposing team's basket. After three missed shots we managed to convince him of his mistake. When our laughter subsided, we initiated our best play. This involved Dean standing on the running track above the basket, receiving a throw and dropping the ball through the hoop. In my senior year the Buff's had lost every game and qualified for the 'Loser's Tournament' to be played in the big house Williams Arena on the Minneapolis campus. I was student teaching and I have always regretted that I did not drive back to campus to help the team in their effort to lose one final game!

Our *AgEd Clubbers* co-ed softball team was actually a decent team. In the Saint Paul campus playoffs we had a problem that only three of our women teammates were available meaning we would have to forfeit. Steve and I begged and pleaded with the non-athletic Susan to be our fourth allowing us to have eight players and at least play the game. Steve suggested, "you can stand in right field and Jim will cover for you. You won't even have to touch the ball." "What about batting" Susan retorted? I replied, "You can just stand there and let them strike you out." The reluctant Susan gave in. Our plan was working well at first.

Several hits were to right field I ran over from center and picked them up. But when Susan came up to bat our plan began to unwind. Instead of striking out, the opposing pitcher walked her. Susan angrily walked the line to first base, cast Steve and I an angry glance and said, “Don’t expect me to run, I will not run!” Then she yelled a nasty name at us, which I will not repeat in this narrative. We managed to win that game which qualified us to play in the Minneapolis campus playoff at the famous Bierman Field in Minneapolis. At Bierman a week later we were facing a team that was talented and they even had uniforms. We managed to keep the score close. Down by two runs, we had bases loaded with two outs when Steve hit a line drive shot up the gap in the middle. Jack was on second base where in his attempt to miss the ball he did a perfect spread eagle jump. The ball hit him in a very ‘vulnerable place’ and he collapsed to the ground. The opposing team tagged him out thus ending our rally. As Jack lay on the ground in pain, Susan gave us an angry scowl, “we have plans for children in our future and if Jack is permanently injured, I’ll never forgive you.” She also said another nasty word in our direction. Steve and I were doubled over with laughter enough to ignore her ire. This event helped us to give Jack the moniker, “Rally Killer!”

During our senior year we joined a former high school friend Brian in an off-campus apartment. Steve initiated a prank on Brian’s bedside lamp. Once a week he would secretly insert a slightly lower wattage light bulb resulting in dimmer and dimmer illumination. Brian fumbled with the light switch and grumbled that something was wrong with the lamp. From my bed in our shared room, I could only pull the covers up and try to conceal my giggling. After several weeks Steve reversed course and began to insert more powerful bulbs. When he reached a two-hundred-watt bulb the jig was up. The previously unsuspecting Brian figured out the prank and shouted, “YOU GUYS!” Great friends, wonderful times and terrific memories of days gone by. We are older now, but we can still laugh like immature kids at the memories!

29 A Clear and Present Danger!

My only excuse is that a movie theatre can be really dark after the film has started!

Charles Shultz the creative genius of the *Peanuts* carton strip often began his stories with the primary character Snoopy, the long-eared Beagle, sitting atop his doghouse with a manual typewriter. The black letters emerged on white paper as he plunked key-by-key paw-by-paw the ominous words in preface, 'It Was a Dark and Stormy Night!' Well, it was a dark and stormy night, the kind of night where I decided to imitate Humphrey Bogart by rolling up my collar and state in a low husky voice "Here's looking at you kid!" When that impersonation failed to achieve a positive effect on my wife, I agreed in an act of chivalry to drop her at the door of the Kandi Six movie theatre to keep her out of the rain. While I am a decent listener, I am not always a good information processor. Wiping my glasses and standing in front of the movie marquis I tried to recall Laura's parting words about which movie we would watch. Six critical choices. I immediately ruled out the children's animation and the travel documentary. Another choice was a romance – thriller – action feature, titled something like, *While You Were Sleeping and Snoring, I Bought a Lethal Weapon*. Scratch that one. Too much like reality. I made a cautious decision.

Did Laura say right or was it left side? Have you ever noticed how dark a crowded theatre can be after the movie has started? As I inched my way down the right aisle, I was relieved to recognize the dark coat and short blond hair of my love, with an empty seat saved for me. I plunked down with a sigh and a sideways glance. "Honey, you bought popcorn. What a good idea – you never buy popcorn." As I reached for a handful of the treat, no scene of *Freddy Krueger* or *Friday the 13th* could have completely prepared me for what happened next. The beautiful face of my wife *morphed* into that of a man. "AAAH" – I gasped." The unspeaking mask slowly turned towards me. I managed to splutter, "I- I- I'm sorry. I thought you were my wife." The face continued to turn with a steely eyed, unblinking stare. I managed to compose myself enough to state, "You know, I don't think there is anything I could say right now that will make this any better, so I think I will just get up and leave."

Laura would later report that she found me wandering in the lobby with a sort of shocked-glazed look on my face. “Where have you been? What are you doing? The movie is almost half over.” I think I mumbled something in reply, “popcorn… right side… dark theatre…umm...nowhere…nothing!”

A Clear and Present Danger proved to be a pretty decent movie. I’m still not certain how Jack Ryan got down to Columbia. Going to have to watch the full version next time. I have to say, that I was fairly impressed when he pulled out his CIA credit card and purchased a twelve-million-dollar Huey Helicopter. All to perform an emergency soldier rescue. Just think of it, 12.5 million Reward miles!

It was not until we were on our way home that evening and I had extracted several verbal promises of extreme confidentiality, that I confessed the true reason I was tardy to the movie. I have since learned that verbal confidentiality promises are not binding. Although I must say that the retelling of a good yarn and excessive hilarity can be a bonding experience to one’s children and friends.

New York Times Bestselling Author Michael Perry stated in his book *Roughneck Grace*, “I wish there was some moral to this story other than don’t be me.” He makes a good point. With a bit of humor, my Dark and Stormy Night seems just a bit brighter.

Postscript: My children love to bring this story up to dinner guests. My wife became a choir director in the small town of Lakefield. She had no directing experience, but people turned out in force after she began sharing tales of my misadventures. There was the threatening motorcycle gang that in actuality turned out to be a skunk. The talking cake pan lid that was begging me to cut and eat a piece of double chocolate with fudge frosting. That incident got a strong dose of laughter. Those were all good anecdotes, but my dark and stormy night was a crowd pleaser that really brought down the house!

30 Boundaries.

When the storm strikes there are limited physical and personal boundaries!

The New London Story Show topic 'Boundaries' was announced and I considered an incident that fit the topic. I was thinking about a recent experience where I stood with my hat in my hand staring across the international boundary with Canada. Addy, our current and 3rd golden retriever, had had enough of the long bumpy journey down the two ruts that led through miles of woods and ended at the upper reaches of the Pigeon River. When I opened the rear hatch of my SUV she made a break for amnesty by escaping across the river to the Canadian side. Should I go after her? The Canadian Mounties could not possibly leave this section of the border unguarded, could they? I imagined security cameras and Mounty hats behind every tree and rock across the way. This dilemma prompted some memories of other boundary issues I have faced in my life.

On the first trip with our 1967 lemon yellow Chevrolet station wagon, I was convinced the engineers had made a serious design error. The rear seat was created with exactly 31 vertical ribs. Even as a youngster I knew enough math to recognize that you could not divide 31 ribs into equal halves. Thus the middle rib of the seat was considered a sort of imaginary boundary line. My sister stated, "If your arm crosses that line, I am going to cut it off and it will be mine forever." I was quick to test the boundary by sliding a pinky finger across the middle rib and shouting "mom – dad, Mary Beth is chopping off my finger. Make her stop!" I upped the ante by accusing, "Mary Beth is sliding her foot on my side of the line." And we continued this boundary conflict for miles upon miles.

A trip to the Boundary Waters Canoe Area thirty-five years ago, found us in 98-degree humid weather, which is unusual for the very northern tip of Minnesota, even in August. We didn't think too much about that, but we did use our blow-up air mattresses to float in the Alpine Lake bathtub like water which may have been a bad idea for my air mattress in retrospect. Just before bedtime, I pulled our Alumacraft canoe up onto shore, tipped it upside down as a place for Sunny our Golden Retriever to sleep.

That evening when my back was turned, our first golden, Sunny, stole our plate of fish and swallowed it in a single gulp. Somewhat later she began coughing and choking. When an amazing amount of foam started coming out of her mouth Laura exclaimed, “She’s choking on a fish bone!” Miles from a veterinarian we were on our own. I had been versed in first aid and I decided to administer the Heimlich maneuver. “It must be stuck in her throat,” I gasped. I managed to straddle Sunny’s back and administer several upward thrusts to her stomach. Nothing but more foam. I considered giving mouth to mouth. Nope, too much slimy foam, not going to cross that boundary even if she is my best friend! I decided instead to give stronger Heimlich thrusts and asked Laura to pry Sunny’s mouth open while I did so. This time success! Out popped not a fish bone, but a toxic, foamy, slimy, giant Toad! Sunny walked away indignant that we had robbed her of her prize. We laughed ourselves to sleep thinking about our hard-mouthed dog who was unwilling to give up her foul-tasting Toad!

Sometime during the night we began to hear thunder in the distance. As the storm moved closer, we were hearing crashes with ever increasing intensity. Safe inside our twenty-dollar Pamida tent I was not alarmed at the steady downpour of rain, until the intensity grew. I have been to a water park where a giant water tank tips and you are essentially drowned in a 500-gallon deluge. Well that was our storm except that it didn’t stop, just a continuous downpour. We could hear trees falling and lightning crashing near us and it was frightening. Then my problems really began. My air mattress went flat. (don’t they always seem to do this at the worst possible time?) The floor of the tent had two inches of water on the level and it was rising at an alarming rate. Meanwhile Sunny’s bed under the canoe was now a part of the lake and she decided to climb under the rainfly of the tent. This effectively flattened it on my side. I whined to Laura, “The tent wall is collapsed, my air mattress is flat, and I am lying in two inches of water!” Laura’s response was as chill as a boundary line drawn across the floor space. “My side of the tent is fine, I’m still dry –

stay on your side. If you come over here, you will pop my air mattress too!"

Somehow, we made it through the night. We rose to dense fog, waterlogged clothes, saturated food, and a floating canoe. Fortunately, it was saved from escape by my last-minute attached security rope. The water had risen over three feet and our campsite was no longer land – but lake. We dumped everything into the canoe and made for what we imagined was the direction of the portage. Except it was not there. What was 'there' were hundreds of fallen trees spanning what used to be our portage. The path had become a rushing stream of water and the whole thing looked, well, impossible.

When we finally traversed everything across, we realized that Sunny, the water dog, was having none of it. She refused to budge from the beginning of the trail. No number of treats could coax her to step foot into the rushing river. So in the end we reached an unequal compromise. I carried her across and then considered eating one of her treats as my own reward. Hey! The package stated that they were made from real bacon. When the final leg of our trip across the 4,000 acres and 100 islands of Seagull Lake confronted us completely blanketed in fog with maybe ten feet of visibility, we followed our compass. I am somewhat proud that we did not accidentally end up across the border into Canada. After hours of paddling, we arrived at our vehicle, kissed the ground, and returned to civilization. We later learned that the area had received over 8 inches of rain and tornado force winds during the night.

Have you heard the joke about what happens when you play a country western song backwards? You get your wife, money and truck back! The Jim song is my escaped dog comes back, the fried fish is delicious, we have a better tent with bulletproof air mattresses, and I am no longer lost in the woods. My conflict with Canada is resolved, the line across the bottom of the tent has been erased and Laura and I are back on good terms. All Boundaries have been restored!

31 Anesthesia

Shiloh loved electrical wires of all types!

The sign on the wall of the surgery center flashed a warning, "All who enter this room will receive a new knee and be sent home with a puppy." The trouble with anesthesia is that the effect is so sudden there is hardly time to appreciate the experience. As I drifted off, I recall pondering... "Wait – What? A PUPPY???" and then blink I was out. For you to fully understand the significance of this moment I need to back up the story a bit with a bit. Our first pet was a cute Golden Retriever puppy which we picked on a beautiful sunshiny Minnesota Spring Day and so she was named "Sunny." We had read that the Retriever is affectionate, friendly, obedient and eager to please, but can be stubborn, easily bored, may have body odor, and are copious shedders. Like many newlyweds love helped us to overlook the negative and embrace the positive. I do want to clarify here; I am not talking about my spouse in puppy love, just puppy dog-puppy love. At the same time in life we acquired a kitten. The jet-black Kato would wait for Sunny to nap and race from hiding and pounce on the unsuspecting sleeper. Or carefully climb on her back and sharpen his claws. The kitten would often crawl under the dog's muzzle, firmly attaching all four paws from below. Sunny would awaken in surprise and furiously bat a front paw at Kato all the while swinging the firmly attached kitten back and forth. They were friends, it was great fun and I have never experienced anything like it again!

Our second canine was a Yellow Labrador. My seven-year-old son named him *Shiloh* after a book that he was reading. Author Phyllis Reynolds Naylor should have included a chapter in her book about how *Shiloh* could dig giant holes in his owner's yard, large enough that two boys could disappear in them. She should have mentioned that the dog was obsessed with electrical wires and could take the wiring harness off a car and trailer in a heartbeat, then chew them into tiny four-inch pieces you could swear were cut with a snip. Phyllis might have included a chapter where the father comes home and receives an ominous greeting "You better listen to the answering machine." The breathless message from our neighbors to the North, "Our Christmas decorations have been stolen, most likely by some high school pranksters. We noticed that yours are gone as well. We are calling the sheriff; do you want us to report your vandalism too?" *Shiloh's* owner (let's call him Jim) hastily calls the neighbor and pleads with them to hold off on the law enforcement call – give him a moment to check something. Sure enough, he discovers an enormous, neatly clipped pile of what were formerly Christmas lights, a slightly disheveled wreath, a mostly deflated Santa Claus and all wrapped up like a package with a neat orange electrical cord. A few weeks later our neighbor to the South reported (with greatly exaggerated hilarity in my opinion), "Hey! I saw the funniest thing on the road in front of your house the other day. A big yellow dog running down the street dragging what must have been one hundred yards of Christmas lights, and Santa did not appear to be enjoying the experience!" Of course, none of this was in the book, but don't you think real life experience is more interesting than fiction? When my wife surmised that *Shiloh* was lonesome, and his behavior would improve with a companion we acquired *Sage*. *Sage* was a smaller Golden Retriever and mostly a great addition to our family with one exception, she took great pleasure in tormenting the larger lumbering *Shiloh* by not allowing him to eat. I could place food dishes on opposite sides of our one-acre property – but Sage somehow managed to race between the two dishes relentlessly guarding both. She was not really interested in eating, but apparently gained pleasure from not allowing *Shiloh* access to food either.

All in all, our pets have given us a great deal of pleasure, but you know the drill. One year of our life is the equivalent of seven dog years. So at roughly seventy years of age *Sunny* left us, *Shiloh* met a tragic end on highway 23, and finally *Sage* developed a brain tumor. The veterinarian came to our home to mercifully put an end to her trauma. As *Sage* looked at us with her big brown eyes the Veterinarian, Laura, and I had tears in our own. I decided, no more pets for me! I can't let another one come into my heart and then experience the pain of letting them go.

It is hard to think rationally with your arms attached to yards of surgical tubing while lying prone on a gurney with your backside mostly exposed to the world. (I just want to stop here and elucidate for the record) What kind of a twisted person invented the one size fits all, 'small' tie in the back, hospital gown? In that state there was a mostly one-sided conversation with my daughter Emily and wife Laura about a litter of *Hunter's Golden Puppies* that were going to be available soon. Was there really a sign on the wall? Or maybe it was just a drug induced euphoria? In any event I nodded in the affirmative. I would be starting over! I announced that we should name the puppy *Anesthesia*! And you guessed it, I was quickly overruled.

A few months later *Addy* and my new knee were standing in a circle with other pets and people in the Willmar Civic Center enrolled in an obedience class. When the instructor asked me point blank if I had read the course instructions, I sort of gave a foot shuffling response to her question, "Umm." She then prodded, "Is this a six-foot-long leash?" With downcast eyes I responded that "no, it appears to be more of a three-foot-long leash." At this point it was explained that the directions were clear, and I had not read them. In a no-nonsense tone she informed me that I had better find something six foot in length before the next week's session. In any event, inadvertently we became "targets" for the remainder of the course. I must say we gained a great deal from the experience. *Addy* had great fun playing with the other dogs and I had several one-sided interludes with the instructor. One friend, a classmate as well as a pet expert concluded in a very kind tone, "Jim, *Addy* is really smart." Knowing that, I have finally figured out what she wants. She will sit for hours in my old red pickup truck knowing that eventually I will take her for a ride. Our assortment of pets has really enriched our lives, but I still do not intend to make any more important decisions while under the influence of anesthesia!

32 Crazy Woman

The "crazies" describe more than just
a Montana mountain range!

The envelope contained a letter with words that would change my life. Your services will no longer be needed at Ridgewater College. As is clearly stated in the administrator contract, no reason needed to be given for this action. The words were clear enough, but my mind had difficulty comprehending them. How could my thirty-two years of a career in agriculture education be over? High school agriculture instructor, adult farm management teacher, and most recently regional director of 18 counties and almost 1,000 farm families enrolled. I had just been named the MN Agriculture Educator of The Year! I was hurt, confused, and needed some time to figure out what to do. So Laura had a plan- a retreat to Montana.

We arrived at Hailstone Ranch and our cabin to a note suggesting that the owners had turned in for the evening. “Make yourselves at home,” it read, which we did. As a full moon rose above us, we enjoyed a picnic dinner on the Montana Ranch Cabin Porch, marveling at the silhouette of unending prairie to the east, the Beartooth Range of Yellowstone Park to the South and the Crazy Mountain Range immediately to our West. Backlit by stars, silhouetted with moonlight and punctuated by the darkness of the impressive landform, I began to unwind.

The following morning, we were greeted by Barbara and Lee Langhus. “Welcome to the Hailstone Ranch, explore and make yourselves at home. This is a working ranch, over eleven thousand acres,” Lee explained. “My grandfather homesteaded the main ranch. About one half mile up the valley, right at the foot of the mountain. Do you recognize the scene?” As I turned to admire the homestead, apparently my inward response was not visible enough on the outside. “Yes, recognize it!” exclaimed Barbara with waving hands to emphasize her point. “The Double-Divide Ranch, the opening scenes of the best horse movie of all time were filmed here, Robert Redford in the *Horse Whisperer*, surely you have seen it?” I nodded signifying agreement even as I grasped the beauty of the vista unfolding in front of us. Barbara continued, “Lee’s brother lives on the homestead. Our home and the Ranch Cabin at this location were built here when Lee and I were married."

I noted that while Barbara looked like a rancher, she sounded a bit more like she was from the German Heritage of Stearns County, Minnesota, which I thought was out of place. I took a breath and asked with a feigned innocence, "So you're not from around here? Your home and the cabin appear to be fairly new. Been married a long time?" "Munich Germany" Barbara explained. "I was Chief Executive Officer of one of the largest Marketing Corporations in Munich, Germany. Hundreds of employees were under my command. Then came nine-one-one, the stock market crash and the dot-com recession. My position required that I dismiss and release most of my friends and associates. I performed admirably, and then I crashed into a deep dark depression."

Barbara went on to explain that her sister is the one who saved her. She decided that I needed to get away from the city where I could find myself. The internet provided the answer, a hunter's cabin in the least populated county -fifty people- in the United States. It was not this cabin, but one higher up the mountain above the main ranch which we rented for the entire summer. "There was a lot of room and time for reflection up there."

She explained that after a few weeks she started walking and then jogging to restore her body. "So, there I was, running down the two tracks of Timber Creek Road, right over there," she pointed. "I was straining up the hill in front of me, when a man on a four-wheeler pulled up from behind and stopped me. "Hey lady, you can't run here" he shouted at me. Well I shouted right back. "You can't tell me what to do. I am CEO of one of the largest corporate offices in Munich, and I have checked the maps. This is a public road, and I can run here if I want to!"

The cowboy tipped his hat in agreement that those statements were true enough. "Okay lady, you can keep running if you want to, but just over the top of this hill is a very large bear. At the rate you are going you will come face to face with him in just a few steps. So, you can do that, or you can get on the 4-wheeler and ride up to the ranch with me."

Barbara finished her story by explaining that it was the beginning of a romance with Lee that lasted. "I didn't go back to Munich at the end of the summer but chose to stay here and become a ranch wife. We married and I have found peace and a new life here. We built this house and the Ranch Cabin rental as my idea. An opportunity to continue to use my internet and marketing skills even out here in the middle of nowhere."

It was on our return trip home when it occurred to me that my journey had changed. I was not exactly sure how, but I was confident that just like Barbara Langhus, my new life was going to be okay. In the beauty and solitude of the west, at the foothill of the Crazy Mountain Range, I learned a lesson from a 'not so crazy' ranch wife. Maybe not the same as before, but I would find myself again.

POSTSCRIPT: VIGNETTES OF RANDOM RANCH DISCUSSIONS

Discussion with wife:
"Did you notice that on google maps these mountains are labeled as the Crazies Mountain Range? But on the old map it is called Crazy Woman Mountain." Is this political correctness at work?"

Barbara Langhus:
"Robert Redford, standing almost on this exact spot. Here on this ranch. My girlfriends back in Munich have a hard time understanding my ranch life, but they totally get Robert Redford. Can you imagine? I mean I love my Lee – and he loves me, but just think – what if it had been Redford on that 4-wheeler? I mean whoo-whee! Crazy! He is one gorgeous man."

Letter to Department of Tourism, North Dakota:
Dear Sirs, I would like to suggest a new slogan for your tourism marketing efforts. "North Dakota, 400 miles of not much to see, but there certainly is a lot of room to think!"

Lee Langhus:
"You must be pretty handy with a grill? Yesterday we had our annual cattle sale. A whole year's finances based on one auction sale. After it was done, I was exhausted and went to bed early. Barbara has had me on an all-vegetarian diet now for the last two weeks. Trying to get me healthy. So last night the breeze off the mountain came right across your pork chops on the grill and into our bedroom window. The smell was inescapable and overpowering. I wasn't certain if I should shoot you through the window or come out and ask if I could join you." Me: "I have a couple of them left in the refrigerator and I can keep a secret!"

My discussion with wife:
"Do you remember the 1970's movie Jeremiah Johnson? Based, on the true story of this mountain?" I continued, "What would possess a mountain man to abandon his carefree lifestyle of living in a log cabin, hunting, and fishing whenever he wanted to, with no responsibilities at all, only to give all that up to take care of a crazed woman and her neurotic teenage son up on the mountain?" Laura: "You have a problem with that? I think you better shift to 4-wheel drive. With that kind of sentiment our road ahead looks pretty rough!"

33 Hyperthymesia

A “*string*” of memories!

I was listening to an interview on Minnesota Public Radio and the speaker was discussing a syndrome called Hyperthymesia. What I learned is that a person with this condition can recall an exact memory of any day of their life. Is this me I pondered? As I considered that thought, it brought to mind that my mother frequently agonized about how an uncle plucked a gray hair from her head during her twelfth birthday party and proceeded to tease her about it. Then there was her story about company who stopped for a surprise visit and the bed was not made. The guests ribbed my mother mercilessly about it. She once held hands with a boy cousin on the way home from school and then had to endure the teasing from a pair of bachelor brothers who happened to catch a glimpse of the innocence of childhood. Mom reciting over thanksgiving dinner "I'll pass on having a dinner roll," Wayne Bennet said, "you can have bread anytime. Why fill up on it when you can have turkey, mashed potatoes, and gravy!" She recounted each memory with such regularity that my children started making bets as to how long it would take at each holiday before grandma would recite her stories. The following excerpts may not exactly be *Hyperthymesia*, but they are memories that flash back to me with regularity.

Memory: I grab the juice pitcher by the lid and make it about halfway to the counter before the pitcher dropped away from the top and soundly hit the floor. The grape juice inside the container exploded in an upward motion similar to the pattern of a nuclear bomb. Two quarts of deep purple grape juice covered the freshly painted ceiling, new window treatments, and kitchen wallpaper. It got the tablecloth and the new carpeting that my fiancé was so proud of. In a panic I got on my hands and knees and began sopping up the purple stain with paper, cloth towels and any type of rag I could lay my hands on. To say I was in a state of panic is an understatement! I was on my hands and knees when Laura came through the door and saw the aftermath of my error. She sat down and started laughing. In retrospect I think it would have been better for me if she had yelled at me. That is what I deserved. Poor Laura, the kitchen was never the same. Some nights I still have a nightmare where I am on my hands and knees trying to soak up an endless flow of grape juice, but the flood is beyond my control. I wake up in a cold sweat.

Memory: I am standing on the stage at Northrup Auditorium on the University of Minnesota Minneapolis Campus. It is Greek Week and the men of the St. Paul Campus FarmHouse Fraternity have partnered with the women of Delta Phi on the Minneapolis campus. The stated goal is to win the coveted Greek Week Award. All of the men are wearing striped bib overalls, red checkered shirts with straw hats while the women were mimicking Daisy of the popular *Dukes of Hazard* Tv show. My friends Steve, Jack, and I were placed in the very back row where we managed to dance and sing to the choreography of the *YMCA* and *Look for the Union Label* songs. There were other competitions including a quiz bowl where my friend Steve and his female partners excelled. In any event, the FarmHouse Delta Phi partnership won the trophy. It was then, however, that I learned the real purpose of the partnership. Winning the trophy was not the objective. It was to meet women who might be persuaded to date the men of FarmHouse. Of course it was! Why didn't I think of that?

Memory: My cousin Tom finished a final test on a Friday morning on the St. Paul Campus. I picked him up with my Camaro and we drove straight through seven hours to the very tip of the Gunflint trail. We portaged and paddled our hearts out to join Tom's family at the ultra-beautiful Lake Gillis. My cousin John had prepared fresh lake trout with morrell mushrooms and a side dish of fried potatoes. My aunt Betty handed me a cup of hot coffee and we watched the sun set across the lake above a sheer granite cliff. A pair of loons were engaging in a mating ritual by calling and skittering across the still glass surfaced water. My cousin John uttered words aloud that have followed me all these years. "Ah... the Lake Gillis House is certainly fine this evening." We all lifted our coffee cups in an emphatic toast, "To the Gillis House!"

Memory: Laura was in the dentist chair with five-year-old Matthew standing by her side. The office is an open format with several dental patients in other chairs and hygienists caring for them. Matthew chose that moment to blurt at the top of his lungs "YOU KNOW, MY MOM HAS A BABY IN HER TUMMY AND POISEN IVY ON HER BUTT!" This revelation brought the dentist to a standstill and the rest of the room broke out in resounding laughter. "Yes," Laura explained red faced, "It's true! What can I say except that I am very uncomfortable with the physical and now emotional affects."

Memory: Barb Swanson was providing a violin lesson to seven-year-old Matthew. I am in the room as parents in the *Suzuki teaching method* are required to do. During an appropriate pause he tells his teacher "My dad said that when I play the violin it is like I am sticking a knife between his ribs and twisting it!" (I attempted to explain that Matthew was not trying during his practice time resulting in a horrible squeaking scratching rendition of *A Soldiers Joy*.) Mrs. Swanson was not impressed, and she replied, "I don't think that is the type of encouragement that I am expecting from you Jim." I was clearly in Barb's 'doghouse' and not likely to be getting out any time soon. Of course Matthew earned a superior rating when he played *Soldiers Joy* for his festival judging.

Memory: Six-year-old Andrea Westby is playing in our front yard after her parents dropped her off to go to son Brian's football game. She was playing and it seemed as if she had a sudden prompting to race across the yard and give her father Gary a goodbye hug. That squeeze would indeed have to last a lifetime as Gary lost his life in a tragic auto accident on the way to the game. A few years later young Brian, Ben, Adam, Steven and Andrea lost their mother to cancer. The Westby family has responded to this tragedy with courage and grace beyond measure. I remember Gary and Cindy and I love this family. Hyperthymesia can be a mixed blessing of laughter and tears.

34 Earthquake!

I saved my family from the earthquake, but who could protect them from their father's mishaps!

One Sunday a guest preacher talked about how he would daydream that he was Superman. At a critical moment in the dream, he described that he would sweep in, put his life on the line, and save his family from disaster. It was an interesting homily, and it captivated my imagination. What would I be willing to do to save my own? Like most fathers I am always ready to give advice and sometimes it has been useful to my spouse and offspring. On the other hand, this good old dad sometimes misses the mark.

We had given our children a zip line for the play area in our large yard. I found two oak trees strategically situated for the cable. By holding the handle the kids could have a gradual glide sideways across our yard. When I became the owner of a nice pallet of old wood it seemed perfect for building a tree house. As the project progressed our plans grew more and more grandiose. In short order we had a nice sized deck located twenty feet up in one of our ash trees. The platform had an external ladder and a secret trap door. We decided to add a roof of translucent green plastic and half of the elevated area was enclosed with a slingshot window. Let me share a secret with you. The fun of a tree house is not having a tree house to play in, it is the enjoyment of building it together. The best part is the planning, constructing, and appreciating the results. So when Matthew suggested it would be fun if the zip line was attached to the secret escape hatch, I was all in. He could imagine making a fast emergency exit when his friends were over to play. I proceeded to move the cable to the new location. When the change was complete Matthew climbed up into the tree house to test out the new system. Looking at my work he suggested "I don't know dad, it looks kind of scary." I confidently replied, "don't worry I will stand down at the bottom and catch you." I then spoke the fateful words that I now regret, "you can trust me!" with that encouragement Matthew grabbed the handle and began his downward glide. He started slowly enough but began picking up speed about halfway down the cable. Then the unimaginable happened; his speed increased faster than I had estimated. When I raised my arms to catch him, he zoomed right on past. The glider handle hit the end of the cable with such force that Matthew flew straight out. The power of it broke his grip and he fell six feet to the earth. It appeared that he landed on his neck and head. I ran to his side and in a breathless voice asked, “are you alright?” Matthew looked up at me and said, “who are you?” In the meantime, Laura had been observing the whole episode and came running up to our side. I stated with a bit of growing alarm, ”stop fooling around, are you okay?” Matthew lay on the ground and looked up at me “I feel really dizzy and sick.” We decided that we should take our son to the emergency room. Matthew ended up spending the night in the hospital with a concussion. Feeling extremely bad about my error in judgement, I kept apologizing to him. The nurses brought in a cart with a PlayStation on it with many choices of electronic games. Matthew’s best friend Daniel came to the hospital and joined Matthew on the bed. They were having a great time. The following day Matthew was able to return home, but he took a week off from school to recover from his injury. I’m glad he was okay, but in the future whenever I asked him to ‘Trust me’ Matthew would quickly reply “I did that once and I’m not going to do it again.” It was really hard for me to accept this comment. You should be able to trust your father and protector, right?

Which brings me to the earthquake. I had purchased an old Bethany pop up camper for one hundred dollars. The canvas was a faded brown, and the interior was decorated with a gold and plaid maroon floral print that was typical of the nineteen seventies. But it had a solid frame and was camp worthy. My intent was that we could travel as a family to Estes Park Colorado. Christopher, our youngest was just a baby and it provided a safe place to sleep off the ground. Our old blue minivan had had a propensity for trouble but so far so good until we hit Central Nebraska. The fuel pump failed on a remote section of highway on a day where temperatures reached one hundred degrees. It seemed funny that Emily, Matthew, and Christopher were excited to ride in a tow truck. The same fuel pump failed again a week later in St. Cloud. I rented paddle boats at

George Lake Park for Emily, Matthew and friend Andrea to kill time while my mom and sister brought me a rescue car. Back on the road we had to shelter in a McDonalds because of a tornado warning. I breathed a sigh of relief when we made it to my conference and hotel destination in St. Louis Park.

The following summer we camped at Jay Cooke State Park just south of Duluth and Andrea was with us on this adventure. The Bethany camper was supported by jacks under each corner of the trailer to provide stability while people were inside. Each side had a bench seat with a table in the middle. The table could fold down to make a bed for an additional sleeping area. So, there we were, Emily and Andrea on one side and Laura and I on the other. Christopher and Matthew were sleepers in the middle. It was almost perfect in my opinion. The people that I loved so much together enjoying a hike to the swinging bridge over the St. Louis River. Then a campfire with a hobo pie dinner cooked in the coals from our campfire. Then a bedtime story and us all sleeping together. It is a memory that will remain etched in my mind forever. So how did this perfect trip end in disaster you might ask? I was dreaming these thoughts when the earthquake hit our poor old Bethany Camper. With an urgent yell I called out "Earthquake!" I grabbed Laura and in an adrenaline-fueled moment pulled her from her inside berth, over me and down into the middle sleeping area next to Christopher and Matthew. I then rolled my body on top of them to protect them from whatever debris would be crashing down upon them. To say that my family awoke surprised might be an understatement of my life and possibly my family as well. There was no earthquake, but the rear jacks under the camper had broken dropping us two feet and allowing us to roll backwards until we hit a concrete curb and shuddered to a stop. We were all safe from the experience. I think my family should appreciate that I was willing to sacrifice my body to protect them in their sleep, don't you?

35 Oh! Oh!

Our family vacations have been disastrously memorable!

For many, a favorite vacation memory includes the photographs, and sights and sounds of their experience. My family recounts each trip with the disaster that occurred. If we kept a travel journal each experience would start with a statement such as "Do you remember the blizzard and spending four days stranded in Bismarck? We watched *Cupcake Wars* for thirty-six hours straight!" The punch line was delivered with some jest and love "well that was a fun one!" Recalling each episode brings a chill to my body and a smile to my face.

All I can say is that my disaster habits started early. My dad loved his big canvas tent, but mold had reduced it to a leaky well-ventilated roof. When rain was predicted my dad diligently covered the tent with a sheet of plastic. The inevitable monsoon led to wet sleeping bags and every possession we had brought along. I recall one particular trip where we were required to weather in the group shelter at Gooseberry State Park. When we returned to our soggy tent, dad pulled on the plastic to drain the water that had collected and nearly collapsed our structure. The deluge ran down dad's neck and soaked him completely. He was wet like a duck but never lost his cool.

When my friend Bruce was getting married, we planned a BWCA camping trip for his bachelor party. Another friend Kyle pleaded to join us at the last minute, and I was charged with packing his clothes into our gear pack. It was below freezing cold at night and even snowed some on that trip. Unfortunately, I left a good portion of Kyle's clothes out of the pack by mistake. I think he nearly froze to the bone and begged to go home early. Bruce and I were not sympathetic, and he had to tough it out by staying wrapped in his sleeping bag most of the trip.

Laura and I made a circle route camping trip and one of our stops included a campground near St. Ignace, Michigan. When a motorcycle gang set up camp across from our tent, we were wary but not alarmed. During the night we heard rustling and noise near our picnic table and gear. Laura woke me up and said, "Don't you think you ought to go out there and do something?" To which I responded, "I'm not going out there. Let them steal our stuff, that would be better than getting beat up or even worse, shot." Laura gave a kind of disgusted snort and said, "well if you are not going out, I'm going to do it!" Laura whipped open the tent zipper. After a few seconds she zipped it shut even more quickly. "Our marauder is a skunk!" she sheepishly replied. We both lay back on our sleeping bags and laughed ourselves to sleep.

We entered in a canoe race on the Minnesota River at the behest of our friends Paul and Lori Garding. They wanted to ensure that they would not come in last! With what would be best described as a canoe version of the *Titanic* we fell behind early. When we arrived at the finish line two hours after the last contestants, Laura somewhat seriously questioned my competitive drive. I might have had some doubts myself!

I drove our car into a parking garage in downtown Duluth. The bicycles on the roof did not follow us but lay in a tangled mess on the sidewalk to the gasps of an emerging crowd of gawkers. Oops, I forgot they were there. Fortunately, Duluth had fully stocked Schwinn and Fuji bicycle repair shops. A few hundred dollars later we were back on the road to circle Lake Superior. I surmised it was worth the expense and enjoyed a most memorable ride around the lakeshore of Mackinac Island.

My friends the Schroeder family accompanied us to a BWCA campsite which happened to be the home of a herbarium of garter snakes. Marcia Schroeder was deathly afraid of reptiles. The rest of the party including her husband and children managed to hide and quickly remove any evidence of snakes. Marcia was completely unaware of her campsite companions until the trip was over.

We spent an evening with numerous other people in the bathroom storm shelter in Whitewater State Park. This time we were accompanied by Kasey O'Brien who was deathly afraid of stormy weather. The storm passed but the fright stayed with us for the rest of the evening.

Beth Lake in the BWCA has a perfect cliff for a ten foot jump off into the lake. When Andrea, Emily, Matthew, and I took the canoe across the lake to the cliff we perfectly aligned with a heavy downpour of rain. No problem, we are already planning to swim so does it really matter if we are wet? We enjoyed several daredevil jumps and returned to our campsite. No harm except the stress we caused Laura back at the campsite with no way to communicate that we were okay and having a blast!

There were twisted ankles, missed baseball games and plenty of other adventure stories to mark each journey but when the kids were old enough, we decided that a ski adventure to Bozeman would be just the thing. My mother was adamantly opposed to us going. What if you run into a blizzard or get buried under an avalanche? My response brought my brother in-law Mitch to tears of mirth when I replied, "when we get to a blizzard we will just keep driving and driving and driving until it gets worse and then we will drive some more!" Now so many years later I wish I could apologize to my mom for this inappropriate retort.

We made eleven ski trips on consecutive years as a Christmas break vacation. There was one exception year where we waited till March because of a broken arm which Matthew obtained on a boy scout ski adventure at Powder Ridge. On these adventures we experienced a road hazard ruptured tire in Bismarck, a broken gas cap and fumes in Billings. A closed rest area resulted in an urgent Sunday morning rest stop to a 'trailer house bar' in Custer Montana, total town size less than five buildings. On one adventure the ski lift did not start running until the temperatures rose to -20F. We then braved the cold and made the Bozeman Daily Chronicle. *"Crazy Minnesotan's Brave the Cold to Ski Bridger Bowl."* We were frozen and famous!

On our last ski trip west we were joined by our future daughter in-law Jenna. The long drive home from Bozeman to Minnesota began on New Year's eve. I say began because somewhere between Brandon and Fergus

Falls, Minnesota the alternator on our Chevrolet Trailblazer failed and we were stranded along the freeway with no lights. It was dangerous and frightening. From somewhere in the back, I heard a small voice "I don't think this has ever happened to me before." Welcome to the family adventure, Jenna! The tow truck took us to a hotel in Fergus Falls where we were fortunate to get two rooms for the night. I saw a sign in the lobby for *Big Dukes* Airport Shuttle Service. Duke agreed to give us a ride home to New London on New Year's morning. The family insisted that I ride in the front where I was regaled with stories of Duke's first, second and third wives. I made encouraging comments regarding the problems and insecurities of his life. I almost kissed the ground of our driveway when we were safely home. That same day my good friends Robert Moeller and Ben Pattison brought a pickup and flatbed trailer to give the Trailblazer a ride home to a repair shop. Not many days later we traded for a better model. No more old cars for us – we now own a brand new Suburu Outback adventure vehicle!

I guess the statement "Oh – Oh" and "we can smile about it now" really seem to fit the Molenaar vacation adventures. Ah! for sweet memories and a patient family!

36 Cigar Box Symphony

1870 – 2020

LAKE FLORIDA
MISSION COVENANT CHURCH

The Lake Florida Church has all the attributes of a Holy place!

My fifth grade teacher suggested that I showed signs of potential but spent an excessive amount of time daydreaming. That was a true statement then, but I wonder what Mrs. Vick would think if she could see me now. I have driven past countless intended destinations while thinking deeply about something else. Most of the stories in this book were crafted while I was in a business meeting or driving a car. Lately, I have been daydreaming about my Great Grandfather Gadney, a gifted machinist, creative woodworker and musician. My mother told me that he made musical instruments out of old cigar boxes. Not the flimsy cardboard boxes of today but solid wood rectangular shaped works of creative illustrations and artwork. The cigar box symphony is an idea that has been a random thought in the background of my mind for several years now. What if all the people of my life could come together with these instruments? The daydream seems an appropriate metaphor to conclude the stories of a one-time farm boy.

In my younger days I was filled with a sense of longing for a grandfather. Most of my friends and acquaintances had them and they seemed to have a great deal of fun together. My close neighbor and best friend Tom had his grandpa, Will DeRuyter, who lived on the same farm site. As most of my classmates were farm kids, most had grandpas living close by. My paternal grandfather Harry Molenaar Senior passed away suddenly on a cattle buying trip with his brother in South Dakota. My maternal grandfather Edwin died an untimely death during the great depression. He was a skilled machinist and very musically talented man. My mother recounted that he played the pump organ at the Lake Florida Mission Covenant Church. He would often sing and play the piano in the parlor in their home. Besides hymns he loved the jolly tune *Maple Leaf Rag*. In his memory my sister Mary Beth and my son Matthew have played this song wonderfully as well. Unfortunately, no one talked about his premature death or the circumstances that led to him taking his own life. The untimely loss of father's changed my parent's lives in a dramatic and tragic manner. My dad became the stand in parent and a farmer, much too young. My mom's college dream was ended at that moment of her father's death. How did they persevere through such difficult times?

In the summer of 1982 I was beginning my second year as a high school agriculture instructor at St. Peter Minnesota. I was at the county fair helping my FFA officers prepare to offer a farm safety demonstration when my teaching partner and good friend Cletus Janni walked up to me and said, "Jim you better come with me, you need to call home immediately." This was before cellular phones, so I drove to my apartment and made the call. "It's dad," mom said. "He was electrocuted this afternoon," she told me with emotion in her voice. "Electrocuted" I replied in shock. "Is he in the hospital?" I asked. "No, he's gone" she answered. The drive home that late afternoon was surreal, full of the beauty of an August summer evening, but my mind was racing with questions and denial. We somehow managed to take care of the animals and crops that fall thanks to the help of my Uncle Vernon and our hired man George Dykema. It was a difficult time but somehow, we got through it.

My mother was with us for almost every birthday, holiday, and celebration during the thirty-seven years that followed. One of her favorite memories was of her paternal grandfather John Gadney creating musical instruments out of old cigar boxes. My aunt Loretta recalled that they were string instruments, banjos, guitars, fiddles, dulcimers, and just about any instrument that you could make with a box and some old piano wire. Mom shared that "he and his brothers and my dad would just get together and play music just for the joy of it." She recounted that the whole family would sing and play in the family living room for hours and hours.

The Lake Florida Mission Covenant Church, illustrated by my sister, is the final resting place for so many dear people. At my mother's funeral the pastor described the numerous shade trees set on a hill with an iconic view of water to the east as one the ancient Jewish people would describe as a 'Holy Place.' The church building has been preserved as a place of worship. It is not hard for me to imagine us gathered in this small white chapel to join in music and worship. It would be in this place that a cigar box symphony could easily become reality.

I gave my life to Jesus in a spring fed ice cold swimming pond baptism at Camden State Park near Marshall. It was important to me to dedicate my life to Jesus. It also gave me the assurance that when it is my time I will come before God and then live in His presence. This is not because I have earned it, it is because of His grace. I am certain that a future in Heaven will be a paradise. In my daydreams I can imagine what it will be like.

My father will be camping with a canvas tent and he will have time for fishing. Mom will be delighting us with one of her favorite stories. Grandfather Harry Sr. will return home from a trip out west with pockets full of candy for his children. We will have Ivel's lemonade and cookies, while we enjoy some of Grandma Esther's lefse. Great Aunt Anna will be passing out red hard rock candy. George Dykema will be driving the corn picking tractor and I will be bringing wagons to him on a glorious fall day. My great grandfather John will have passed out cigar box musical instruments and Grandfather Edwin will lead us in playing them in a symphony to the tune of the *Maple Leaf Rag.* There will be joyous singing and laughter! All of the people that I have known and those that came before me will join in the Cigar Box Symphony!

Understand that the cigar box symphony is not just a legacy of the people of the past. It is a love story for future generations. It will be a great day when I can meet you and we can join together in whatever gives you joy. So to all in the future, I hope you will learn about and welcome Jesus into your life as that is the way to enter into Heaven. Then the cigar box symphony will be beyond anything that we can imagine. This is the conclusion of my True Tales, but I hope you realize that this is not the end of my story – it is just the beginning!

Acknowledgements

My wife Laura and children, Emily (Ben), Matthew (Jenna), Christopher (Megan), my sister MaryBeth (Mitch) and niece Erin (Zach), thank you. You have listened carefully and given me encouragement. I appreciate your patience when I have driven past your intended destination while thinking of something else. Thank you, my dear aunts who are still with us and I love you – Doris, Gretchen, Joan, Grace, and May, for putting up with my questions regarding your childhood times. I have so many wonderful friends who have been gracious to listen to my stories. To my best man Kent, and all of my cousins I want you to know that you are important to me.

I owe thanks to the following for encouragement in this project:
*Heather Westberg King, director of the New London Story Show and my editor.
*Joe Garding for an even more careful and precise final edit.
*Kristin Allen, my art instructor and my friends in the Tuesday Evening Drawing Club. It is where I have spent six years learning how to draw the illustrations for this book.
*My friends Brent and Robin Olson for providing a fine example of writing, speaking and friendship that I hope to emulate.
*Mr. Vern Thompson English Composition Teacher at Willmar Junior College who taught me that writing is not so much inspiration but hard work and perspiration. He was right!
*So many friends who have supported me and listened to my stories.
*To those of you choosing to read my short stories, I hope you enjoy the experience!

Jim Molenaar

About The Author

Jim Molenaar is a one-time farm boy raising his own pigs and cattle to finance a college education. He has a wide variety of experiences with farm families during his forty-three-year career in agriculture education. In his early career Jim was a high school agriculture instructor and FFA Advisor. As his career progressed, he transitioned to work as a farm business management instructor (one-on-one education with farmers), farm mediator, farm succession/transition education specialist, MDA Minnesota Department of Agriculture Rural Finance Authority Board Member and Farm Advocate. Jim was instrumental in seeking grants and legislative funding, as well as the initial program design leading to the creation of the Minnesota Rural Mental Health Program for farm families. Over his career he has been recognized as the Minnesota Young Agriculture Instructor, and later the Minnesota Outstanding Agriculture Educator. He was also awarded the Minnesota and National Honorary State Degrees. In 2014 Jim was inducted into the Minnesota FFA Hall of Fame. Jim and his wife Laura have been married for forty years and are parents of three grown children. Jim and his sister Mary Beth still own Section 25 Holland Township land from where these stories began.

Made in the USA
Columbia, SC
02 June 2025

58760726R00089